THE LAST DAYS
OF DON JUAN

First published in 1990 by Absolute Classics, an imprint of
Absolute Press, 14 Widcombe Crescent, Bath, England

© Nick Dear

Series Editor: Giles Croft

Cover and text design: Ian Middleton

Photoset and printed by WBC Print, Bristol
Bound by W.H. Ware & Son, Clevedon

ISBN 0 948230 00 0

THE LAST DAYS
OF DON JUAN

Tirso de Molina

Adapted by Nick Dear

b s o l u t e   c l a s s i c s

INTRODUCTION

Many plays, poems, and operas have been written about the legendary Don Juan, but Tirso de Molina's EL BURLADOR DE SEVILLA was the first. However, the history of this play is vague. We don't know precisely when it was written, though sometime between 1616 and 1625 seems likely; nor do we know for sure that Tirso de Molina wrote it. There are two surviving versions in Spanish, each attributed to different authors. We know very little about when the play was performed, or by whom. Since the first production, a vast number of permutations of the story have been attempted, yet still the Don Juan show rolls on.

It seems to me that the mythic qualities of Don Juan himself are greater than the individual plays, or questions of authorship or authenticity – he survives the new versions of each century, and continues to fascinate and appal. So, when the Royal Shakespeare Company asked me to write an adaptation of the original play, I felt I had ample justification for taking textual liberties, which is exactly what I've done. In changing some elements of the story – expanding the female characters' roles, for example – I do no more than follow a long and rather glorious tradition. Also, it's good fun.

Aside from the great creation of the trickster at its centre, the play survives, I think, largely because of its delight in the comic macabre. It is a very religious play, written by a monk, and designed to demonstrative that Christians cannot count on the last-minute reprieve which confession may seem to offer. It states that there is a point at which God's mercy turns to justice. You have to go with this, for I suspect that to undermine the theological elements of the story – a series of beliefs which I do not share – would be to belittle its dramatic power. It is based on the notion that hell exists, and if you're a bastard, you'll go there. No room for debate. Yet at the same time the play's young characters have such enthusiasm for life, for sensuality, for danger, for the individual spirit, that the conflict between two ways of living throws up some good jokes, and the crucial dynamic of the play.

There is one other reason why the popularity of this story persists, in my opinion. It is that it suggests retribution for the wicked, against the odds. Even as the villain is blithely getting away with it, and all seem powerless to stop him, some greater power intervenes, and sets the world to right. This often seems hard to credit; indeed a few years ago I would have found it hard to script. Yet, as I began work on THE LAST DAYS OF DON JUAN, at the end of the 1980s, the impossible happened – the Berlin wall came down, the dictator of Romania fell, Eastern Europe seemed to find a voice. Some kind of collective desire on the part of the people became so strong as to be irresistible, as is happening in South Africa as I write. It is a time of tempered optimism across the globe – if not, perhaps, in the atavistic underworld of Tory Britain – and for once it seems just believable that the bad guys might get their come-uppance.

NICK DEAR
February 1990

NOTE: This text incorporates changes as they occurred during rehearsal.

THE LAST DAYS OF DON JUAN was given its British première in this version by the Royal Shakespeare Company at the Swan Theatre, Stratford in 1990. The cast was as follows:

DON JUAN TENORIO	Linus Roache
ISABELLA	Julie Saunders
KING OF NAPLES	Raymond Bowers
DON PEDRO TENORIO	Ciaran Hinds
RIPIO	Lloyd Hutchinson
OCTAVIO	Clarence Smith
TISBEA	Katrina Levon
CATALINA	Sally Dexter
ANFRISO	Grant Thatcher
CORIDON	Ross Harvey
BELISA	Polly Kemp
KING OF CASTILE	Michael Gardiner
DON GONZALO OF ULLOA	Sylvester Morand
DON DIEGO TENORIO	David Killick
MARQUIS OF MOTA	Paterson Joseph
DONA ANNA	Yolanda Vasquez
BATRICIO	George Anton
AMINTA	Catherine White
GASENO	Raymond Bowers
MARIA	Polly Kemp

GUARDS, COURTIERS, MUSICIANS, SINGERS, PROSTITUTES, PEASANTS, SERVANTS, ETC. . . .
Georgiana Dacombe, Rowena King, Simon Austin, Stephen Casey, Bernard Wright

DIRECTOR	Danny Boyle
DESIGNER	Kandia Cook
LITERAL TRANSLATION	Kate Littlewood

ACT ONE

SCENE ONE

The play is set in Naples and Spain in the 1620s.
Italy. The palace of the King of Naples. A hot, dark night. Two young
bodies clutching at each other in a corner: Don Juan and Isabella. They
moan with passion. They subside. Don Juan immediately gets up and
starts to dress.

ISABELLA: Must you go, Octavio?

DON JUAN: Yes, but Duchess, I swear I'm yours.

ISABELLA: And everything you've promised will come true?

DON JUAN: Yes.

ISABELLA: Every wish, every dream, every desire will come true?

DON JUAN: We will be married. I have sworn. Which way's the door?

ISABELLA: Wait while I fetch a light.

DON JUAN: A light? Why a light?

ISABELLA: So I may see the face I shall live with all the days of my life. My darling – just let me bring a torch –

DON JUAN: No! I'll torch you if you do!

ISABELLA: What? Shame on your harsh words! . . . Octavio? . . . *(She reaches out to him. He moves away.)* Mother of God, who *are* you?

DON JUAN: A man with no name.

ISABELLA: Duke Octavio is gentle. You are not . . . *(Screams)* Guards! Guards! An intruder!

DON JUAN: Isabella, be quiet –

ISABELLA: Help! Arrest him! *(He tries to kiss her.)* Don't touch me! Filth!

Enter the King of Naples with a candle.

KING OF
NAPLES: Who's there?

ISABELLA: The King! Merciful God!

KING OF
NAPLES: What's going on?

DON JUAN: What do you think? A man, a woman, in the dark, naked – any ideas?

The King puts out his candle.

KING OF
NAPLES: *(Aside)* The kind of affair I would rather not see. – Guards! The Palace Guard, quick!

ISABELLA: *(Weeping)* Disgrace, disgrace!

Enter Don Pedro Tenorio and guards.

DON PEDRO: Sire!

KING OF
NAPLES: Identify yourself!

DON PEDRO: Don Pedro Tenorio, Ambassador of Seville! I heard shouts in your apartments. Who is it?

KING OF
NAPLES: I have no light. I cannot tell. I suspect young people, lurking in the gloom. You investigate. Find out who they are, and take whatever action you think appropriate. And Don Pedro –

DON PEDRO: Sire?

KING OF
NAPLES: I was not here. I saw no scandal.

DON PEDRO: Sire.

Exit the King. Don Juan makes a move to escape.

Hold him.

DON JUAN: Try it! Who's first? My life's not cheap – who'll pay the price?

DON PEDRO: Kill him.

DON JUAN: I want to die – a death with honour! I am a nobleman of Spain, attached to the Embassy. This grants me the right to take you one by one in single fight. Come on!

DON PEDRO: Stay back! – Secure the woman in the next chamber. Go!

> *The Guards chase Isabella and capture her. They lead her off.*

Now, young man. Just you and me. Let's see how hard you really are.

DON JUAN: I am as hard as stone. I could grind you down to dust, uncle.

DON PEDRO: What is your name?

DON JUAN: *(Steps into the light.)* I am your nephew. Like I said.

DON PEDRO: *(Aside)* Hell! This means danger. Explain yourself, you reckless boy! How'd you get inside the palace? And tell the truth, for whatever you say, you're dead.

DON JUAN: Dear uncle, you were my age once. Don't tell me you never fell in love. Remember what it felt like – desperate passion – perhaps you'll understand the risks I took. The truth is that I came here in disguise and had the Duchess Isabella.

DON PEDRO: You seduced her? How?

DON JUAN: I passed myself off as Duke Octavio.

DON PEDRO: Oh, God. . . !

DON JUAN: And under cover of darkness I –

DON PEDRO: Don't go on! I have no wish to know! *(Aside)* It's a whirlpool! If the King hears this, I'm finished. – You pulled the same stunt back in Spain! Wasn't one noble virgin enough? Why must you spread your shame to Naples, and a girl of even higher social rank? God rot you! Your father smuggled you out of Seville to save your useless hide. He gave you a fresh chance as an envoy, and how do you repay him? You slink round like a dog, ravaging the local aristocracy! What the hell are we going to do?

DON JUAN: Little point in saying sorry.

DON PEDRO: Very little point!

DON JUAN: Still . . . You are my father's brother. My blood is yours to do with as you will. Kill me and settle the debt.

Don Juan kneels and offers Don Pedro his sword.

DON PEDRO: Get up, get up, that doesn't help! The family name's still sullied! But you said a fine thing just then. We are kin. And yes, I was like you once. But if it was me, I'd've had more courage, I'd've shinned up to that balcony and been over the wall by now . . .

DON JUAN: I'm a good climber.

DON PEDRO: Well get climbing, then! Slip away, hide yourself! Milan, or Sicily!

DON JUAN: Milan!

DON PEDRO: Good choice! I will send to you there, and relate the outcome of this miserable night.

DON JUAN: *(Aside)* Let's hope every night's as miserable as this. – It's all my fault we're in such trouble, uncle, and I'm dreadfully sorry.

DON PEDRO: Your sin is to be young, Don Juan. Now jump! And God go with you.

DON JUAN: Yes! *(Aside)* Straight back to Seville . . .

Exit Don Juan. Enter the King of Naples, cautiously.

DON PEDRO: Sire! I followed your orders, but the man –

KING OF
NAPLES: Died?

DON PEDRO: Escaped.

KING OF
NAPLES: Escaped? – Fatally wounded?

DON PEDRO: No. He fought like a demon from hell, sire, his cape wrapped round his arm, and though your Guards attacked with vigour, he beat back their slashing blades. His death looked certain. Until he spied that balcony above. His eyes flashed flame. Unearthly flame. I shudder to tell it . . .

KING OF
NAPLES: What was he?

DON PEDRO: I do not know. He flew up to the ledge like a bat to its cave. And before the Guards could reach him, he leapt over the wall and was gone.

KING OF
NAPLES: Dear Lord, protect us.

They cross themselves.

DON PEDRO: Meanwhile the woman – it's the Duchess Isabella, by the way – broke down and confessed.

KING OF
NAPLES: I didn't hear that.

DON PEDRO: *(Loudly)* I said the Duchess Isabella has confessed. She claims the interloper was the Duke Octavio, who, by some sharp stratagem, gained entry, and enjoyed her.

KING OF
NAPLES: Guards! Bring her before me. How little we must value our honour, that we leave it in women's care.

Enter Guards with Isabella.

KING OF
NAPLES: What crazed alignment of the planets, what vile unchristian urge compels you to defile my home with your lascivious beauty?

ISABELLA: Sire, I was tricked, I –

KING OF
NAPLES: Silence! No female logic can excuse your disgusting crime. So it was Octavio, was it?

ISABELLA: Oh Sire, I –

KING OF
NAPLES: One would have thought that with the number of bars, bolts, cannon and sentries at one's command, one could keep out this troublesome lust. Yet our defences have been pierced by a devious boy. Don Pedro, throw this whore in a dungeon, and then arrest the Duke. He shall learn that pleasure must be paid for – at the altar.

ISABELLA: Your Highness, I beg you, look me in the eye.

KING OF
NAPLES: Your fornication you hid behind my back. It now
              seems apt to turn my back on you.

                   Exit the King.

DON PEDRO: This way, please, Duchess.

ISABELLA: *(Aside)* I have fallen from grace. I have sinned. My
              reputation lies in tatters, among my petticoats. Why is
              it always we who take the blame? They think this was
              Octavio. Let them do so. If he still will accept me, I
              am not completely lost.

                   They exit.

SCENE TWO

Italy. Enter Duke Octavio and Ripio.

RIPIO: You are up early, sir!

OCTAVIO: Who can sleep when his heart's on fire? Love is a
              child, Ripio. He hates to be tucked up in bed. He
              loathes soft linen sheets and lacy eiderdowns. He lies
              there with his eyes wide open, longing for the dawn,
              and light enough to rise and play. Oh, I am a child
              again! And these thoughts of Isabella keep me from my
              rest. They gnaw at my night-time soul, and make my
              body suffer – how I ache for her! But I stay pure. And
              guard her virtue. Wherever she may be.

RIPIO: Sounds bloody stupid to me.

OCTAVIO: What do you mean, stupid?

RIPIO: Stupid as in daft.

OCTAVIO: Explain yourself, idiot.

RIPIO: Your love, sir, is ridiculous.

OCTAVIO: Thank you. Do go on.

RIPIO: This girl. Does she love you?

OCTAVIO: Why of course she does!

RIPIO: And you love her?

OCTAVIO: I do.

RIPIO: Well, if you was me, I would not let myself be driven
             half mad by some bird I was in love with who loved
             me back in return with compound interest. If she was
             cool – if she was giving you the elbow – if she looked
             the other way when you came by, and gobbed at passing
             children – I might counsel flattery, presents, and
             sleepless nights strumming your guitar. However, if
             you worship her and she worships you, don't muck
             about, get married.

OCTAVIO: Fool! Where's the romance in that? Weddings are for
             slaves and washerwomen.

RIPIO: Nothing wrong with a nice wet washerwoman.
             Spreading out her laundry in the sun. Scrubbing her
             smalls in a steam-bath. Kind and generous people, do
             anything for a bloke in need. Not like some I could
             mention. You should try slipping her a bar of soap, and
             see what happens.

             Enter Don Pedro and Guards.

OCTAVIO: Sir?

DON PEDRO: Sir, Don Pedro Tenorio, Ambassador of Spain.

OCTAVIO: Sir.

DON PEDRO: Sir.

             They bow to each other.

             You sleep late, Duke Octavio. Your conscience must be
             clear.

OCTAVIO: When your Excellency comes calling it would be wrong
             to sleep at all. Indeed, now I have made your
             acquaintance I shall stay awake for ever. Yet you visit
             rather early in the day. . . ?

DON PEDRO: I carry the King's commission.

OCTAVIO: If I linger but an instant in the thoughts of the King, I
             am honoured. Were His Gracious Majesty to ask for
             my life he would have it. What good fortune brings you
             here from him?

             Don Pedro dismisses the Guards.

DON PEDRO: Ill fortune, my lord Duke.

OCTAVIO: Not possible.

DON PEDRO: A warrant for your arrest.

OCTAVIO: My arrest? Who accuses me? What is the charge?

DON PEDRO: Surely you need no explanation? – Well, for what it's
             worth, this is my theory. Very late last night I found
             myself in consultation with the King – affairs of state –
             you know how the powerful hate the hours of sunlight.
             Suddenly we heard a woman scream! The carved
             ceilings of the palace echoed with her cries! The alarm
             was rung, the King and I sped to the rescue, and what
             do you think we found? Eh? Fair Isabella in the arms
             of some strong brute, some lustful dog who dared to
             disregard the royal curfew. His Majesty ordered the
             lecher's arrest. I had him outnumbered and back to
             the wall, when all at once he sprang, three storeys high,
             and shrieked, and breathing fire and tar and dust
             absconded through the darkness! It was as if the Devil
             himself appeared, here in Naples! We spoke to the
             Duchess then, who solemnly declared it was you,
             Octavio, who had defiled her.

OCTAVIO: I dare you to repeat that!

DON PEDRO: In public, she said it in public! With her knickers
             round her knees! I'm only telling you what the whole
             world is already –

OCTAVIO: That's enough! I can stand to hear no more of
             Isabella's treachery! (Aside) But maybe it's a trick. –
             Tell me the rest, then. Come on, speak up. When and
             where and what positions. . . . Your silence poisons my
             heart! But my resolve will never weaken. You are a sly
             one, sir. How do I know you're not merely spouting
             gossip? Is it possible my love could leave me, in full
             knowledge I will die? Yes. It is. I slide from happy
             dream to gaunt reality. . . . No! She is constant! I will
             not doubt! Don Pedro, did she deceive me? Did I put
             my trust in a mirage? Damn the woman! She makes a
             mockery of love, a mockery of honour! She whose
             chastity I've sworn to protect . . . swimming in some

foul man's sweat . . . clutched in his arms. . . . Dear God, is it true?

DON PEDRO: Just as birds fly, fish swim, four elements make up a man, and if you pray you go to heaven, it's true.

OCTAVIO: I simply can't believe it! That she should turn out to be no more than a woman! My Isabella!

DON PEDRO: Yes. What the hell are you going to do? The King is furious.

OCTAVIO: Though I am innocent, I had better run away!

DON PEDRO: I agree. I like you, Octavio. Slip out through the back.

OCTAVIO: Thank you, Don Pedro! – Ripio! Pack!

RIPIO: Yes, sir!

    Exit Ripio.

OCTAVIO: Oh reed that bends with every gust of wind, I fly from your deceit; I leave my native land, and you, and follow my sad fortune. Farewell, Italy! *(Aside)* Isabel stolen by some lewd thief? God, I will go mad with grief!

    Exit Octavio. Don Pedro pauses to breathe a long, satisfied sigh of relief, then exits.

SCENE THREE

Spain. A seashore. Enter Tisbea, with a fishing pole.

TISBEA: Of all the girls who live along this shore,
Of all the girls who play in the curling waves,
Of all the girls of Tarragona, whose rose
And jasmine feet dance in the hot, white sand –
I am the only one
Untouched by love.

Here, where the sun wakes
And creeps across the sea, lighting
Sapphire-blue peaks on the water;
Here where every grain of sand's a pearl,
A particle of sunshine;
Here is where I live.
I hear the romance of the sea-birds, the cries

Of dippers and waders,
The sighs of the waves on the rocks,
And I feel not a lick
Of desire.

My fishing pole is my greatest joy.
This supple rod, that whips and bends
With the wriggles of hooked fishes.
Some days I take my net and snare the crabs
And shellfish of the shady pools, dark places
Thick with mystery. For I'm at peace.
The serpent tongue of love's unknown to me.
My heart is free.

When my girlfriends and I set sail in a skiff
Upon the raging ocean,
They tell me of their aching hearts, hot dreams,
Infatuations.
Well, I have to laugh.
Poor victims of love.

Love hunts for me but I slip his nets.
I sleep on in my simple hut;
The danger passes over.
I like my hut, it's a
Cathedral of thatch, with a spire of smoke,
A choir of bright cicadas. In there
My virtue is preserved in straw,
Like ripe fruit, or
Delicate crystal.

The brave Tarragonian fishermen, who defend
Our coast from pirates,
All fancy me to death.
But I reject them, every one.
They make such crude suggestions.
I find it a help to go suddenly deaf
And turn to stone, for then
They quit their advances
And leave me alone.

Anfriso is the nicest.
The muscles on him – goodness!
He speaks well, he can read and write, he's brave,
He gives to beggars. If things go bad for Anfriso,

He just carries on filleting flatfish, shrugs,
And grins his grin.
A truly lovely man! But –
Hangs round my cottage in all weathers.
Leaves poems pinned on trees.
Starves himself.
I see him out there shivering, in icy wind
And rain, playing his pan-pipes right
Through the night, just for me!
Only for me!

I ignore him, of course.
I am a tyrant, aren't I?

The other girls can sigh for him, and die for him,
And drown themselves in perfume, but I,
His chosen, give him naught but pain.
This is love's triumph.
To never know when you are beaten.
To clutch at empty air.
To adore where despised
And despise where adored.
To wound, humiliate and – oh! What a waste
Of breath, to talk of love
When you could be fishing –
Please, just leave me to bait my hook
With a squirming worm or a lump of squid,
And cast far out to –
Look! What's that?

A sinking ship!
Sails like a peacock's tail, fanned out
With pomp and pride!
But it's struck the reef, bound for the bottom!
Two people have leaped overboard!
Down goes the hulk with a roar!
Now only the tip of the mainmast's left –
The wind in the topsail thrashing
Like a wild thing locked in a cage!
Now one of them's carrying the other one, swimming
So bravely through the surf – they've gone down!
No, they surface!
They're gaining the shore!
They're sucked under!

Please God, don't let those people die!
(Calls) Anfriso! A shipwreck!
Coridon, Alfredo!
Come quick, help the survivors!

Exit Tisbea. Enter from the sea Catalina carrying Don Juan.

CATALINA: Someone, give us a drink of wine! The sea's far too damn salty. I don't mind a little salt with my eggs, but this is absurd! Not only could you drown out there, you could end up pickled as well! All right if you like sardines, I suppose, but I don't. You'd've thought God would've had the sense to mix a little white wine with his ocean – make it more palatable for the drowning. I can't stand water at the best of times – but salted water! Ugh! . . . Master? Oh Lord, he's cold as ice! Master! Wake up! – Like a wet rag. Is he dead? The sea done this, but knowing my luck, I'll swing for it. Bleeding stupid idea, putting bits of old wood on the water, and expecting them to float. As for that damn needle they spend so much time staring at, with the little N at one end and the little S at the other, well, if that's what they used for their canvas, no wonder the sails blew away! And now look at us! Shipwrecked!

Enter Tisbea.

TISBEA: Good woman, are you still alive?

CATALINA: I am. He's not.

TISBEA: He is, he's breathing!

CATALINA: Breathing? Where from?

TISBEA: Why, here, through his nose, of course! Where else does it come from?

CATALINA: You'd be surprised. – You're too pretty. Keep away.

TISBEA: What are you saying? The poor man's ill. Quick, go and call those people from over by the boats. But first, tell me who this fine young gentleman is.

CATALINA: He is the firstborn son of the High Chamberlain to the King of Castile. We are headed for the royal court at Seville.

TISBEA: What is his name?

CATALINA: His name is Don Juan Tenorio.

TISBEA: Don Juan Tenorio . . .

CATALINA: *(Aside)* Oh, God, here we go.

Exit Catalina. Tisbea cradles Don Juan in her lap.

TISBEA: You beautiful boy. Wake up, oh do wake up. . . !

DON JUAN: . . . Where am I?

TISBEA: Safe in my arms. The danger's over.

DON JUAN: I must have died and gone to heaven. . . ! – for my head's laid in your bosom, after the nightmare of the sea. I've swum from hell to paradise! And you, are you an angel? You have the face of one. You have the skin of velvet, the hands like fluttering wings. . . . Some dreadful whirlwind wrecked my ship and threw me at your feet, but in this fate has intervened, for now I know what I did not, that I was born to love you.

TISBEA: You've a lot of chat in you for one who was half-drowned. Must be the shock.

DON JUAN: It is a shock, perfection, a terrible shock.

TISBEA: And you're very saucy, too. Perhaps it's all that sea-water you've swallowed. Here, lie down, let's see if we can pump some out. Oh, my, you are a talker. Slippery, silver words, like eels in the air. I bet you've been rehearsing them, while pretending to be senseless on the beach. *(Aside)* Please God you aren't some wicked liar! Though chilled and wet, you feel like fire! Oh, I burn up! Please God, don't let him be some cold seducer!

DON JUAN: I wish I'd perished in the sea. It would have been less dreadful than this banging in my breast. My heart bursts for you! My passion, madam, knows no rest. You shine like the sun. My body turns to ashes in your heat . . .

TISBEA: Goodness.

DON JUAN: Tell me your desire's the same!

TISBEA :   *(Aside)* I never thought I'd feel this flame! Please God he is not some deceiver!

              Enter Catalina with Anfriso, Coridon, Belisa, and fishing folk.

              Your master is recovering.

DON JUAN :   Your breath awoke the spark of life within me.

ANFRISO :   How can we help, Tisbea?

TISBEA :   These are my friends.

ANFRISO :   I would do anything for you. Command me with those ruby lips, as red as red geraniums, and let me serve you. I'll plough the sea, water the wind, walk on hot coals, broken glass, vipers' nests, anything!

TISBEA :   Why, thank you, Anfriso. *(Aside)* Just yesterday his flattery seemed soft. But suddenly I start to get the picture. – Friends, I was fishing from the rocks, when out to sea a boat capsized and went down by the reef. This brave woman swam ashore, rescuing her master. He's a nobleman. I saw him lying limp in the sand, and look, I have revived him.

CORIDON :   We can see that. What do you want us to do?

TISBEA :   Take them both to my hut. They're important people. We'll mend their clothes, and feed them. Do you like sardines?

CATALINA :   Love 'em.

              Don Juan takes Catalina aside.

DON JUAN :   Come here. – Who are you exactly?

CATALINA :   I'm Catalina, sir. Your cook.

DON JUAN :   Cook? Where are the others? The equerries? The grooms?

CATALINA :   I fear the rest of them are drowned.

DON JUAN :   What? Out of all my retinue, I've no-one but a cook?

CATALINA :   I'm very loyal.

DON JUAN :   If this fishergirl asks about me, don't tell her a thing. She must not know my name!

CATALINA: I wouldn't dream of it. She's very, very pretty.

DON JUAN: Isn't she . . .

CATALINA: Please let me continue to serve you, sir.

DON JUAN: Absolutely gorgeous . . .

CATALINA: I've no other home. I'll do any job. Don't turn me out. I'll starve.

DON JUAN: I owe you my life. I suppose I shall be needing some assistance. I plan to have this little mermaid. Here. Tonight.

CATALINA: I know your tricks, Don Juan. I've seen you at work before. But she's independent-minded. How will you persuade her to –

DON JUAN: Keep quiet and follow me. And get some proper clothes on. You're not decent like that.

CORIDON: Tonight's the night, Anfriso, of the fishermen's fiesta. There'll be wine, goats' meat, and music. What I propose is this: I challenge you to dance. The best dancer wins Tisbea's hand. What do you say?

ANFRISO: You're on!

DON JUAN: Tisbea, help – I'm faint.

TISBEA: Doesn't stop you talking.

DON JUAN: I can barely walk . . .

TISBEA: You're doing all right.

DON JUAN: But feel my brow – my temperature's so high. . . !

TISBEA: *(Aside)* Please God he's not a trickster, or I'll die!

They exit.

SCENE FOUR

The Alcazar at Seville.

Enter the King of Castile and a courtier.

COURTIER: Sire, The Knight Commander Don Gonzalo of Ulloa, Ambassador to Lisbon, is returned.

Don Gonzalo is ushered in, and bows to the King.

KING OF
CASTILE: Welcome to Seville, Commander. Your report?

DON
GONZALO: Sire, I presented my credentials to your royal cousin,
King John of Portugal. I found him in the process of
equipping thirty warships, to attack the Moors at Ceuta
and Tangier.

KING OF
CASTILE: God send him fair weather! I wish him success. Now, did
you agree terms?

DON
GONZALO: Yes, Sire. He requests the following territories: Serpa,
Olivenza, Mora, and Toro. In return he will grant you
all the provinces between Castile and Portugal.

KING OF
CASTILE: Excellent! Sign the treaty. Congratulations, Don Gonzalo.
Splendid work. Now tell me about Lisbon. What's it
like? Nice place?

DON
GONZALO: It is the greatest city in the whole peninsula of Spain.
Shall I describe it to you?

KING OF
CASTILE: Yes, please do.

DON
GONZALO: Lisbon is the eighth wonder of the world!
In the bowels of Spain, in the province of Cuenca,
The mighty River Tagus has its source.
From there it tears our countryside in two,
Flowing swiftly to the sea, streaming lastly
Through the heart of ancient Lisbon.
At the mouth it forms a port
Between two high sierras; here you may see
Ships of all the navies of the world!
Barques, caravels, galleons rigged for war,
Scarred veterans of our American conquests –
All guarded on the westward side, where lies
The vast Atlantic, by two enormous fortresses,
Cascais and St John.

Half a league outside the city, at Belem, you find
The Monastery of St Jerome, containing
The tombs of all the Kings and Queens of Portugal,
And Vasco da Gama, navigator of the globe.
From here the city appears
Like a cluster of jewels, dangled from the sky . . .
The beautiful streets unfold with convents,
Churches and ancestral homes, where noblemen,
Scholars and soldiers live, upholding their
Great laws. But the finest building of all
Is the Misericordia, pride of the city,
And envy of Spain.
From the high towers of this colossal structure
You see no less than sixty towns
Along the sunny coast. Lisbon is ringed
By twelve hundred estates.
The land is fertile, the people content.
The roads are lined with poplar trees.
The orchards drip with nuts and fruit.
Precisely at the centre of the city is the Rossio,
A handsome square, which but a hundred years ago
Was covered by the sea. But the sea,
Succumbing to the pull of some strange tide,
Flowed on, and thirty thousand houses now stand
Proudly in its place.
There is a street called 'Rua Nova' –
'New Street' to you and me –
Full of oriental treasure, where the merchants
Count their money by the sack-full! – according
To the King. He lives in a magnificent residence
Called Terrero. Here is moored an armada from
France, England, the North,
With cargoes of barley and wheat. Wrought in iron
In the gates is the royal coat of arms:
A red sphere at its base to symbolise
The bloody wounds suffered by Alonso Enriquez
In his first crusade for Christ against the Moor.
Most impressive.
In Lisbon you can sit eating supper,
Drinking the sparkling wine,
With the fishermens' nets so close it seems
Your food has vaulted straight from sea to table!
Every night a thousand ships arrive

With rare, exotic goods,
Oils and spices, meat and grain,
Every kind of fruit, and ice
From the hills of Estrella
Which the women sell from baskets on their heads!
But I must end.
To try and mention every detail
Of this glorious location
Would be to try and count the stars
That fill the sky. Let it suffice
That there are living there
One hundred and thirty thousand
Of your loyal Christian subjects,
And a solitary King, who through myself
Would kiss your hand.

KING OF
CASTILE: Splendid! Splendid oratory! Don Gonzalo, you have
             surpassed yourself! Your brief account brings Lisbon to
             life with such colour, such vigour, that listening to your
             description is I'm sure preferable to actually going
             there. Now, I must reward you. Have you any
             children?

DON
GONZALO: Yes, Your Majesty. I have one daughter – Anna.

KING OF
CASTILE: She is beautiful, no doubt?

DON
GONZALO: She is very charming, yes.

KING OF
CASTILE: Then will you permit me to suggest a suitable match?
             It is in my gift.

DON
GONZALO: My family are honoured, Sire. I accept on her behalf.
             Who is to be the husband?

KING OF
CASTILE: We await his return from abroad. A well-placed
             Sevillian, Don Juan Tenorio. Quite a striking boy.

             They exit.

SCENE FIVE

Seashore. Enter Don Juan and Catalina, now wearing a man's clothes.

DON JUAN: See those horses? I want them saddled and standing by.

CATALINA: What? Steal horses? Never. The name of Catalina is a proud and honourable name.

DON JUAN: Certainly is, for such a chicken.

CATALINA: You mean I'm supposed to do your dirty work?

DON JUAN: Correct. Whilst the fishermen are drinking, slip round and borrow their nags.

CATALINA: Borrow? We're bringing them back?

DON JUAN: The fast exit is my signature. I rely on pounding hooves.

CATALINA: Are you really planning to take advantage of the girl who saved your life?

DON JUAN: Seduction is my special skill. I cannot break the habit. I thought you said you knew me. . . ?

CATALINA: I know you're a bastard to women.

DON JUAN: But I'm dying for this sea-nymph! A body like Italian art! Exquisite! I have to possess it!

CATALINA: And once you've possessed it, you're off, are you? That's a fine way to repay her hospitality.

DON JUAN: You are tedious. Don't you remember Aeneas behaving exactly like this towards Dido, Queen of Carthage?

CATALINA: No I don't. When was that?

DON JUAN: . . . Before I was born!

CATALINA: Well, I'm older than you, and I still don't remember.

DON JUAN: Christ, you're old enough to be my mother.

CATALINA: If I was your mother, sir, I'd box your ears for bad behaviour. They say one day you pay, for all your naughtiness on earth, don't they?

DON JUAN: Plenty of time to settle that debt. Meanwhile I'll do what I want.

CATALINA: Well, I'd sooner be me than you. Sooner be called a chicken than have debauchery on my conscience. Here comes the wretched peasant. Wait till she learns the truth. . . !

DON JUAN: Just hitch up the horses.

CATALINA: Poor girl! What payment, for board and lodging! She filled his belly – now he'll fill hers!

Exit Catalina. Enter Tisbea.

TISBEA: Don Juan. . . . I feel all wrong when we're apart. My heart seems dry as dust.

DON JUAN: You're a prick-tease, aren't you, miss?

TISBEA: What?

DON JUAN: You expect me to believe that you can't live without me? What rubbish!

TISBEA: It's true.

DON JUAN: Oh, do you love me?

TISBEA: Yes.

DON JUAN: Do you?

TISBEA: I promise you I do!

DON JUAN: If you did you'd give yourself to me. You'd give me everything.

TISBEA: I will give you everything!

DON JUAN: I want it now. Why hesitate?

TISBEA: Because you are my punishment. I thought I was impregnable. But I love you so hard it hurts.

DON JUAN: I love you too, from the depth of my soul! My life is yours, to throw away or treasure! Haven't I sworn my vow? We'll be married as soon as we find a priest!

TISBEA: I'm not worthy of you.

DON JUAN: How can you say that? You're perfect.

TISBEA: But I am of low birth.

DON JUAN: My darling Tisbea, love cuts across the classes, love's a King, love conquers silk and coarseweave just the same, when we stand together naked we'll be set completely free. . . !

TISBEA: I want to believe you! I want to! But all men are traitors and liars.

DON JUAN: Listen . . . today in the shimmering net of your hair, I was snared like a silly little fish. I'm trapped. I'm yours forever.

TISBEA: And will you be my husband?

DON JUAN: Yes! I swear! Your eyes are the bait, your mouth is the hook . . .

TISBEA: Take me! But remember, God hears you –

DON JUAN: (Aside) Yes, he's heard it all before, actually.

TISBEA: – and judges you at death.

DON JUAN: And until death, I promise you, I live to be your slave. Shake hands. Now we are joined.

TISBEA: Do what you like with me. . . . I'm not shy . . .

DON JUAN: Quick, then, I'm quivering!

TISBEA: Come into my love nest, behind my walls of straw. My pallet will be our bridal couch. Come inside my cave . . .

DON JUAN: Where do I get in?

TISBEA: I'll show you.

DON JUAN: Hurry! I'll explode!

TISBEA: (Aside) Please God, don't let him be a rogue. . . !

They exit. Enter Anfriso, Coridon, Belisa, Musicians.

BELISA: Tisbea! Want to watch the dancing?

ANFRISO: She's so cruel. The man who falls for her gets naught but misery. He just squirms like a lizard on a stick.

CORIDON: Wonder what she's doing now.

BELISA: She's entertaining strangers.

CORIDON: I don't like the look of it.

ANFRISO: You're not the only one. Are we dancing, Coridon?

CORIDON: I'm ready.

BELISA: Play on, then!

Music. The two men dance.

(Sings) A lass went to the ocean for
to fish with nets and poles;
she caught no fish, but hauled ashore
a thousand lovers' souls.

Enter Tisbea, dishevelled.

TISBEA: Fire! Fire! My hut's in flames! My tears won't put
them out! My humble home is burning like a town
destroyed by war! I thought my walls were hard. I
thought I was made of rock. But the fury of love burns
even stone, engulfs my house of straw!

Fetch water! I'm ablaze! Have mercy, love, you scorch
my soul!

My cottage is a place of wickedness. I was deflowered
there – left hot and red and bleeding in that oven of
desire. My guest was false! Oh monstrous boy! He's
stolen my honour, and fled! May the sparks of dying
stars fall on his head, and burn his hair with shame!

Yes, it happened to me! The one that mocked all men.
He came like a cloud in off the sea, and darkened my
nights and my days. Don Juan! – he tricked his way
into my bed. I was so proud! Now I'm nothing.
Disgrace rains down on me.

He even took the horses! I want my revenge! . . . I'll
follow him. I'll walk to Seville. I'll throw myself before
the King, and beg for justice!

Fire! Fire! My soul's on fire! The world's on fire! Fire!

Exit Tisbea.

ANFRISO: I'll go after the brute!

CORIDON: I'll comfort Tisbea. She's desperate. – Well someone
          ought to keep an eye on her.

          Exit Coridon.

BELISA: She should've known better than to have such pride.
          You can't live without love, it's not natural. I knew
          she'd come to a sticky end.

          Enter Coridon.

CORIDON: She's thrown herself into the sea!

ANFRISO: Tisbea! Come back!

BELISA: She's gone mad!

          They exit.

SCENE SIX

*The Alcazar at Seville. Enter the King of Castile and Don Diego
Tenorio. The King is angry.*

DON DIEGO: I'm afraid it's true, Sire. I have received a letter from
            my brother, Don Pedro, your Ambassador to Naples.
            My son Don Juan was discovered cavorting in the
            King's apartments, with a beautiful woman of the
            court.

KING OF
CASTILE: Was she of any importance?

DON DIEGO: The Duchess Isabella?

KING OF
CASTILE: The Duchess Isabella! Good God! She's betrothed to
            the Duke Octavio! This boy of yours is becoming a
            menace. Where is he now?

DON DIEGO: I have to report he's slipped back to Seville.

KING OF
CASTILE: Tenorio, I must tell the King of Naples of your son's
            crime. Send a letter to your brother; we can rely on
            him to put it tactfully. Also, say that I have matched
            Don Juan to Isabella, to help redeem her honour.

Furthermore, as of this moment, Don Juan Tenorio is banished from Seville!

DON DIEGO: Where to?

KING OF
CASTILE: He shall live in Lebrija. He must leave tonight. But what about Don Gonzalo? I had planned to marry Don Juan to his daughter, in thanks for his mission to Lisbon. Can't do that now, can I? To keep Gonzalo in good humour, I shall appoint him Lord High Chamberlain in your stead. You can be his aide.

Enter a Courtier.

COURTIER: A nobleman from Italy is recently arrived at court, Sire.

KING OF
CASTILE: His name?

COURTIER: The Duke Octavio.

KING OF
CASTILE: We will receive him.

Exit Courtier.

DON DIEGO: Sire, my son's a delinquent wretch, and full of cheek. Octavio has been wronged. But for the sake of the good name of Tenorio, I implore you, don't let them fight a duel.

Enter Octavio.

OCTAVIO: Great Majesty, Alphonso of Castile, I fall humbly at your feet. I am a miserable exile without home or fortune. I flee the folly of a woman, and the trespass of a rake. I offer my service to the royal house of Spain.

KING OF
CASTILE: My dear Duke, I already know, as a matter of fact, that you are completely innocent of any evil-doing. I shall write immediately to the King of Naples, and suggest he restore to you your estate and all your holdings. But since you are now here in Seville . . . with your permission, you shall be married, and to a lady beside whom the Duchess Isabella, after what she's done, will seem to you quite ugly. Don Gonzalo of Ulloa, Knight

Commander of Calatrava, Ambassador to Lisbon, Scourge of the Moors, and Lord High Chamberlain of the Palace of the Alcazar, has a daughter, Anna. She is young, virtuous and fair, which should be dowry enough on its own in my opinion, so do not ask for more. She is the brightest star in Seville, and I wish her to be your wife.

OCTAVIO: Sire, if this is your pleasure, it will make all the hardship of my journey worthwhile.

KING OF
CASTILE: Find the Duke accommodation, Don Diego, and ensure his needs are met.

OCTAVIO: Gracious Majesty, my faith in you is well rewarded. Of all the eleven Alphonsos, I count you as the first!

Exit the King and Don Diego. Enter Ripio.

RIPIO: How did it go?

OCTAVIO: Fantastically well! I got everything I wanted, and more besides. I conducted my campaign with real brilliance, Ripio! The King has chosen to arrange my marriage! And he says he'll write to Naples and repeal our banishment.

RIPIO: Famous for his generosity, isn't he? So – got another bird, sir, have we?

OCTAVIO: Yes. I'm to have a Sevillian wife. The men of this proud city are renowned for their boldness and good looks. No doubt they breed fine women, too. Here they cover the dazzling lights of their eyes with a silken veil: the style of Seville. I rather fancy that. By God, I feel happy again!

Enter Don Juan and Catalina.

CATALINA: Hold on, master, there's that Duke, that you left cuckolded in Naples.

DON JUAN: Act normal. Octavio, my dearest friend –

CATALINA: *(Aside)* First the flattery, then the treachery.

DON JUAN: – I was called away from Naples by my King, and left

in such indecent haste, I had no time to bid you
goodbye. Please forgive my disrespect, sir.

OCTAVIO: Sir. It is a day of good fortune. We meet again.

DON JUAN: Who would have thought you would ever have forsaken
the splendours of Italy, which you loved so well? This
behaviour only makes sense, Octavio, in light of the
fact that you left it for Seville.

OCTAVIO: I confess I did not believe your stories, Don Juan, until
I saw your magnificent city with my own eyes. – What
sort of citizen is that?

The Marquis of Mota approaches, with his retinue.

DON JUAN: The Marquis of Mota! – An old acquaintance of mine.
You will not take it as discourtesy if I leave you, to
converse with him?

OCTAVIO: Not at all, my friend. My sword-arm is ever at your
service. *(He bows to Don Juan.)*

CATALINA: *(Aside)* And your women, too, I suppose.

RIPIO: Did you say something?

CATALINA: I said my, er, sword-arm is at your service, too, and my
egg-whisk arm, and my rolling-pin arm . . . if you want
them . . .

Exit Octavio and Ripio. Enter the Marquis of Mota.

MOTA: Don Juan, dear boy, I've tracked you down at last! I
heard you were back, but couldn't find you. Very odd,
I thought. I thought you'd come flying straight to my
side.

DON JUAN: I'm here. Why complain?

CATALINA: *(Aside)* Yes, why not simply hand over whatever's near
and dear – your sweetheart for instance? Then you'll be
sure of his undying brotherhood. That's what I like
about Don Juan: he always behaves as a nobleman
should.

DON JUAN: How's life in Seville?

MOTA: The whole court is changed.

DON JUAN: Any decent women?

MOTA: One or two.

DON JUAN: Ines?

MOTA: Gone to Vejel.

DON JUAN: Charming. Why?

MOTA: Been put out to grass.

DON JUAN: Been put out to die. And Constanza?

MOTA: Losing her hair. Plucks it by the handful.

DON JUAN: But still plucks her eyebrows?

MOTA: Yes!

DON JUAN: And Theodora?

MOTA: Spent the summer sweating out the pox. Putrid. But
             better now. Sent me one of her teeth wrapped in lilies.

DON JUAN: Curious. What about Julia of Candilejo? Does she still
             sell her body for swordfish and trout?

MOTA: You can have her these days for a piece of old cod.
             Smells fairly similar, too.

DON JUAN: I've no doubt. Listen, the district of Cantarranas . . .

MOTA: Yes?

DON JUAN: Is that slum still the place for cheap sex?

MOTA: Some things never change. Last night Pedro Esquivel
             and I stuffed an old tart for nothing.

DON JUAN: What, nothing at all?

MOTA: No! Ran off without paying. Her pimp was incensed!

DON JUAN: Deliciously cruel! What was her name?

MOTA: Beatrice. What a joke, eh? I'm returning tonight to
             perform it again!

DON JUAN: I'm coming too. This carnal talk has made me amorous.
             But what about serious seductions, Mota? The ladies of
             the court?

MOTA: Don't ask.

DON JUAN: Why not?

MOTA: I'm sick with love for one.

DON JUAN: Is it hopeless?

MOTA: It's doomed.

DON JUAN: I see. Not interested.

MOTA: Oh yes, she's hot for me, adores me.

DON JUAN: Then – ?

MOTA: I just can't get near her, that's all. She's my cousin Anna. Been away with her father in Lisbon. Just returned to Seville. Lives in there.

DON JUAN: Good-looking?

MOTA: A masterpiece. Nature's finest creation.

DON JUAN: *(Aside)* I must effect an introduction. – If she's so beautiful and wonderful, Mota, why don't you simply get married?

MOTA: Because the King has matched her to another, dear boy!

DON JUAN: Who?

MOTA: Nobody knows! I'm in agony!

CATALINA: *(Aside)* If he goes on like this, it's his own stupid fault. The great seducer of Spain has started planning his assault!

DON JUAN: Why, you should be the happiest man alive, blessed by the love of such a lady! Let the world fry! Make your move, and to hell with the morals!

MOTA: I am!

DON JUAN: . . . You are what?

MOTA: I've come here to wait around on my own for a bit and try and learn the outcome of her fate.

DON JUAN: Go into the palace and ask. Courage!

MOTA: Ask. . . ? Very well, I shall. Wait here for me.

Exit Mota and retinue.

DON JUAN: Follow him, Catalina. I need to know what happens.

Exit Catalina. Dona Anna appears at a barred window, above.

DONA ANNA: You – what is your name?

DON JUAN: I have no name. Who asks?

DONA ANNA: I hope you can be discreet.

DON JUAN: I assure you I can.

DONA ANNA: You are a friend of the Marquis?

DON JUAN: His closest. Who are you?

DONA ANNA: Please give your friend this letter. – But do be careful, as it contains not only writing, but also a lady's honour.

DON JUAN: In that case, you've chosen the right person. You have my word as a gentleman that this lady's honour will be passed on to Mota intact.

DONA ANNA: I thank you, stranger. God be with you.

Exit Dona Anna.

DON JUAN: Well! What kind of chimera was that? Was it real? Or an illusion? A letter, dropped into my hands like a formal invitation from heaven. For sure, that was the girl the Marquis of Mota has fallen for. You can see why, too. In Seville I am called a seducer and a rogue, and frankly, with good reason – for my great pleasure's to hunt down women and abuse them, and leave them weeping hot tears for their honour. This little one I'll tear open, as soon as I've left the square. But wait – the seal is still wet. *(Laughs)* A skilful intrigue, this. It's come unstuck. Afraid I'll have to read it. Yes, it's signed by Dona Anna, in a round, cultured hand.

"My darling, my brute father has arranged my nuptial mass. I cannot disobey. And yet I cannot live without you. If you love me as keenly as you say, as I so dearly love you, too, come to the courtyard door tonight at eleven o'clock; the maid will let you in. Wear your crimson cloak so she knows you. And cousin, be true, as I am true to you, too, for ever. Your unhappy love – "

(Laughs) Oh dear, oh dear. Stupid girl. I'll take her as I took old Isabella, in the marble halls of Naples . . .

Enter Catalina.

CATALINA: The Marquis is returning – none the wiser.

DON JUAN: Listen, you and I shall be busy tonight.

CATALINA: You've got a new scheme.

DON JUAN: Yes, a colourful one.

CATALINA: Whatever it is, I do not approve.

DON JUAN: We'll get away with it.

CATALINA: We? What do you mean, we? I'm not helping out with your horrible tricks.

DON JUAN: You stole two horses. That's a serious offence.

CATALINA: You think you cheat the world, Don Juan, but you only cheat yourself. Take care. Or you'll end up good and damned, on the Day of Judgement.

DON JUAN: What is this, the Holy Inquisition? How insolent!

CATALINA: The truth makes me brave!

DON JUAN: And fear makes you a coward! I don't need advice. What are you, anyway? Not even a valet. A cook! Advice, from a cook! You have to appreciate that a man gets nowhere without a few risks!

CATALINA: Yes, and the bigger the risk, the worse the punishment when finally they catch you.

DON JUAN: I'm warning you, Catalina! No more sermons! Or you're out – understood?

CATALINA: Someone else will take me in.

DON JUAN: That's hardly very likely. Look at yourself. Not exactly a raving beauty, are we?

CATALINA: I've a good brain.

DON JUAN: That counts for nothing in this town. You stay with me. You need me. Understand?

CATALINA: I understand. I'll follow your orders. *(Aside)* What choice is there? I've nothing to my name. Oh, if I had a little money . . . – What do you want me to do, then? Undress women? Swindle men?

DON JUAN: Shut up. Here comes the Marquis.

CATALINA: *(Aside)* Oh, he's the victim, is he?

             Enter Mota.

DON JUAN: Mota! Whilst you were gone someone whispered a
             message through those bars! I couldn't see properly,
             but it sounded like a beautiful woman.

MOTA: Anna!

DON JUAN: Might it be? She said at midnight precisely you're to go
             to the courtyard gate, and secretly the maid will open
             it, and let you in to taste the spice of illicit flesh. In
             order that they recognise you, my friend, you're to
             wear your crimson cloak.

MOTA: That red cloak I wore to Mass on Sunday?

DON JUAN: That's the one. Midnight, remember. Not before.

MOTA: She whispered this? Didn't write it down?

DON JUAN: She said her father'd confiscated all her paper.

MOTA: Don Juan, this message has renewed my hope!

DON JUAN: Your lips might be better used to kiss your cousin,
             Marquis.

MOTA: Sorry! In my excitement I forget my manners! Oh, let
             it be night! I want to pull down the sun, and make the
             world dark!

DON JUAN: The sun is sinking of its own accord.

MOTA: Then it is time to dress. I return home to investigate
             my wardrobe. I must do something to occupy my
             mind, or I shall go berserk with joy!

DON JUAN: You'll run even wilder at midnight.

MOTA: Dearest boy, thanks to you I have my prize. May God
             reward you for your service to a friend.

DON JUAN: Sir.

             They bow, and the Marquis exits with his retinue.
             Enter Don Diego.

DON DIEGO: Don Juan!

CATALINA: It's your father.

DON JUAN: What can I do for you, sir?

DON DIEGO: You can become saner, wiser, more humane, more honest, and altogether better behaved. And that's just for a start! Is every aspect of your dishonourable youth designed solely to kill me with shame?

DON JUAN: Calm down, your heart will fail. What is it this time?

DON DIEGO: Your idiocy! Your philandering and your lies! For which the King today has had you exiled from Seville! Your evil nature has outraged him. He knows, though you hid it from me, of your conduct at the court of Naples. To betray your closest friend! And in the royal household! You filthy traitor. God alone can find fit punishment for such crimes. You think you live a charmed life, don't you, Juan? But He sees. He sees. And he gains revenge at death.

DON JUAN: Don't make me laugh, old man. I have a lifetime yet.

DON DIEGO: I assure you, it's gone in a trice.

DON JUAN: So where must I languish, to satisfy His Majesty? America? Darkest Peru?

DON DIEGO: Lebrija. – I agree, it's far too lenient, given what you've done.

CATALINA: *(Aside)* Bit of luck he doesn't know about Tisbea.

DON DIEGO: You are to remain in Lebrija until your insult to the Duke Octavio has been repaired. The only way to achieve this and appease the Italians is for you to wed the woman Isabella.

DON JUAN: You mean I have to sleep with her *again*? That's too harsh a discipline, father.

DON DIEGO: . . . Since nothing I can say or do appears to have the slightest influence, I leave you in the hands of God.

Exit Don Diego.

CATALINA: Your poor father. He was upset.

DON JUAN: The old always cry. It's all they have left. Come on – it's getting dark. Time to find the Marquis!

CATALINA: You mean you're throbbing for his woman. Why don't
            they see you coming? Why don't they scent you're on
            heat? You're a locust who preys on virginity; you
            gobble up girls like fresh corn. You should have a
            warning sign, written on your britches: "Caution.
            Deflowerer of maids. Do not be fooled by this man's
            name, he's the greatest cheat in the whole of Spain!"

DON JUAN: I like that. Very catchy.

            They exit.

SCENE SEVEN

*Night. The back alleys of Seville. Prostitutes leaning from windows,
drunks and pimps on the streets. Enter Marquis of Mota with his
guitarists. They play wild, sensual music. Mota dances, grotesquely, with
a prostitute. Others join in.*

SONG: Time passes slowly for lovers who wait
            To meet in the shade by the courtyard gate.

            Enter Don Juan and Catalina.

DON JUAN: Mota!

MOTA: Don Juan!

DON JUAN: I knew you as soon as I saw the red cloak. Where are
            we going?

MOTA: We're going down the Alley of the Snake. We walk as
            Adam walked, proud and erect. For in this dark valley
            lie a thousand sinful Eves, I'm told, who sell
            themselves for apples. Which is a dash good thing as I
            for one ain't taking any money.

CATALINA: I'm not going into that dark place! It's foul! I went
            down there once looking for a restaurant and got a
            pisspot tipped on my head!

DON JUAN: Ignore my servant, who is a weed. You intend to call
            on Beatrice again?

MOTA: No.

DON JUAN: Why not?

MOTA: She's stationed a man outside her door, to beat me up and rob me.

DON JUAN: I'll go in your place.

MOTA: You'll never succeed!

DON JUAN: I'll pretend to be you. I'll speak in your voice. I'll say I've come to settle my dues. They'll let me in, and I'll do it. Fast. The only difficulty will be convincing the pimp that I'm really the Marquis of Mota. If I only looked somewhat more like you . . .

MOTA: I know! I'll lend you my cloak.

DON JUAN: Of course! Why, you are a genius!

MOTA: Suits you, too. Just saunter up and ask for Beatrice. Good luck! We'll meet at midnight.

DON JUAN: Farewell.

MOTA: What a brilliant joke!

CATALINA: Where are we going?

DON JUAN: Shut up.

CATALINA: This isn't it. Beatrice lives down that way.

DON JUAN: Shut up! My plan is rather different.

CATALINA: Ah. I have to admire your audacity.

DON JUAN: Deception, I cannot resist. Come on!

          Exit Don Juan.

CATALINA: I've heard of showing a red rag to a bull, but I've never heard of a bull giving you a lend of the red rag so's you can smuggle yourself into the cowshed and –

          Exit Catalina.

MOTA: I thought of that! It was my scheme! They'll think he's me! We'll trick them! . . . Golly, what a wild, eccentric night this is!

          Exit Mota and the Musicians and Prostitutes, dancing and singing:

SONG: Time passes slowly for lovers who wait
       To meet in the shade by the courtyard gate . . .

SCENE EIGHT

*Outside the Ulloa house. Dona Anna and Don Juan within, in an
embrace. Enter Don Gonzalo outside, with a torch. Light through the
window.*

DONA ANNA: You're not the Marquis! I've been deceived!

DON JUAN: I tell you I am!

DONA ANNA: You lie!

       *Don Juan makes a run for it. Don Gonzalo draws his
       sword.*

DON
GONZALO: That's Anna.

DONA ANNA: Someone kill this traitor! He assaults my honour!

DON
GONZALO: She says she's been dishonoured. Who would dare?

DONA ANNA: Help, he's ruined me!

DON
GONZALO: Don't shout so loud, girl – you ring like a bell!

       Enter Don Juan, with sword drawn.

DONA ANNA: Kill him!

DON
GONZALO: The fortress of my honour, sir, is undermined! The
           walls are breached, the castle is invaded!

DON JUAN: Let me pass.

DON
GONZALO: You can pass on the point of my sword!

       Enter Catalina, with a kitchen knife.

DON JUAN: You'll die.

CATALINA: Don't!

DON
GONZALO: No matter. My good name's already dead.

DON JUAN: I promise you, I'll kill you.

DON
GONZALO: No, *you* die, fraud!

CATALINA: *(Aside)* If I get out of this, I swear I'll never help again, nor take a tip, nor nothing!

>   *Don Gonzalo and Don Juan fight.*

DON
GONZALO: You have cut me mortally!

DON JUAN: You were enraged. You threw away your life.

DON
GONZALO: It was no use to me . . .

DON JUAN: Let's go!

>   *Exit Don Juan and Catalina.*

DON
GONZALO: My blood pumps out in anger. . . ! Coward! Traitor! I die alone. . . . But be warned. My fury pursues you forever!

>   *He dies. Enter Dona Anna.*

DONA ANNA: Father!

>   *Blackout.*

SCENE NINE

Night. Mota alone. A church-bell chimes.

MOTA: Now the clock strikes twelve. Why's he so late? I do hate waiting!

>   *Enter Don Juan and Catalina.*

DON JUAN: Marquis?

MOTA: Juan?

DON JUAN: Yes. Take your cloak.

MOTA: How was the hoax?

DON JUAN: Mortifyingly good.

CATALINA: Fly from the dead one, master! Run!

MOTA: How did you achieve it? What's my alibi?

CATALINA: *(Aside)* You're a prat, what more do you want?

DON JUAN: This joke has proved expensive.

MOTA: I fear I'll pay the price. For I'm the one the woman
            will accuse.

DON JUAN: It's midnight. Farewell.

MOTA: May dawn never come, to chill my pleasure!

CATALINA: *(Aside)* Poor fool! He's no idea!

DON JUAN: Catalina! Quick!

            Exit Don Juan and Catalina. Raised voices, off.

MOTA: Commotion in the Alcazar. What can it be, past
            bedtime? Suddenly I'm cold with fear. A vast array of
            torches! Looks like a blazing Troy! They're coming this
            way, flames streaming out like comets' tails! But
            why. . . ?

            Enter Don Diego Tenorio and guards with torches.

GUARD: There! Him in the red cape!

            They surround Mota.

DON DIEGO: What are you doing on the streets at this hour?

MOTA: Simply trying to discover what the devil's going on.

DON DIEGO: Arrest him!

MOTA: Me? Whatever for? Do you realise you are speaking to
            the Marquis of Mota?

DON DIEGO: Whoever you are, hand over your sword. The King has
            ordered your detention!

MOTA: Dear God! Why?

            Enter the King of Castile and courtiers.

KING OF
CASTILE: I'll search Spain, I'll search Italy, I'll search Portugal, there's nowhere he can hide, I shall find him!

DON DIEGO: Your Majesty, this is the man.

MOTA: Sire, I am innocent, please, why am I arrested?

KING OF
CASTILE: Sever his head and stick it on a pole.

MOTA: *(Aside)* The mystery, the ecstasy of love, so light at first, and then so heavy! The cup of delight I had raised to my lips, and still I spilt it. Drat. The King's jolly frightening when he's angry, isn't he? – Sire, I know not what I've done!

KING OF
CASTILE: You alone know fully what you've done.

DON DIEGO: Move!

MOTA: Whatever I did, it wasn't me!

KING OF
CASTILE: Prosecute him instantly! I want to see the inside of his neck! . . . The Commander shall be buried with solemnity and pomp, the full extent the state affords its most distinguished elders. He was dear to me. He made me laugh. The Knights of Calatrava are diminished by his passing. And all Castile shall grieve. Make him a grand tomb, of bronze and stone, and place on top a statue of the man in all his glory! And underneath this likeness, in an azure blue mosaic, I want it said that vengeance will be his. . . !

              They exit.

SCENE TEN

A stonemason's yard in Seville. The Stonemason and his Mate work on the statue of the Commander, but so far all they've hewn from a huge block of granite are his feet. Enter Dona Anna, in mourning.

DONA ANNA: Those feet . . . I remember them paddling in the river . . . or booting the flanks of your horse . . . I want revenge, Father. I dream of it, I pray for it, I think of nothing else. I will know no peace till the insult is returned. I am witch-like in my purpose, I'll sacrifice to any god, consort with demons, lie with wolves, I'll summon dervishes, astrologers, banshees from the deserts of Arabia, I must know who he was! The man in red. I cut myself, I write in blood, I eat bad meat, I pick through dirt, I beg you, please, dear Father – come back, and take revenge!

Exit Dona Anna. The Masons watch her go, then once more chip away at the stone. . . . And fade.

END OF ACT ONE

ACT TWO

SCENE ONE

The countryside near Dos Hermanas. Church bells ringing. Enter a wedding procession: Batricio and Aminta, her father Gaseno, Maria, shepherds and musicians.

MUSICIANS: *(Sing)* The April sun shines warmly over
Orange blossom, purple clover;
Beautiful, and of good birth,
Aminta's like a sun on earth.

BATRICIO: Let's sit here on this carpet of flowers, where the hoar frost turns to dew. This is my favourite spot.

AMINTA: *(To Musicians.)* Sing a thousand compliments to my beloved husband.

MUSICIANS: *(Sing)* The April sun shines warmly over
Orange blossom, purple clover;
Batricio is the perfect groom –
To his wife's sun, a constant moon.

GASENO: *(Applauding)* Very good singing! Much nicer than that Kyrie we had in church!

BATRICIO: Aminta, compared to your lips, compared to your cheeks, the sun is a dull, flat thing in the sky.

AMINTA: Oh, Batricio, you flatter me. But thank you. If I shine, it is in your light. You are the dawn of my life.

MUSICIANS: *(Sing)* The April sun shines warmly over
Orange blossom, purple clover;
As sun and moon, in harmony,
These lovers find their destiny.

Enter Catalina, in travelling clothes.

CATALINA: Hello, shepherds! Could you do with some extra guests at your wedding breakfast?

GASENO: Everybody's welcome at my table! Who do you bring?

CATALINA: Don Juan Tenorio.

GASENO: Old man Tenorio?

CATALINA: No. His son.

MARIA: A handsome nobleman! I've seen him!

GASENO: Please fetch your master, if Batricio – ?

BATRICIO: *(Aside)* This is an evil omen. My joy turns to jealousy,
            quick as a cloud across the sun. What does a handsome
            nobleman want at my wedding? The devil must have
            sent him down our road! – If he wishes to dine with
            us, I am content. But a Don at a wedding's a very bad
            sign.

            Exit Catalina.

GASENO: Nonsense. Let the Colossos of Rhodes come! Pope
            John! Alphonso the Eleventh, and all his court! They'll
            see how valiant, how generous Gaseno is, who laid on
            this great feast! Why, we've bread stacked in sierras,
            guadalquivirs of wine, babylons of bacon, quail and
            thrush and pigeon ranked in columns of rich meat! Let
            the gentry come to Dos Hermanas, and honour my
            grey hairs!

MARIA: He's here! He's the Lord High Chamberlain's son.

BATRICIO: *(Aside)* So much the worse. He'll want the place of
            honour by the bride. Shite! I've had barely half an
            hour of matrimonial pleasure, and already I'm made
            jealous by my rotten awful luck. This is love, then, is
            it? This suffering in silence?

            Enter Catalina and Don Juan.

CATALINA: Don Juan Tenorio of Seville!

DON JUAN: Good people, one was riding along the road to Lebrija,
            when one heard your wedding bells, and thought, how
            utterly charming – a country saturnalia! One simply
            had to detour off to watch the lusty revels. May I. . . ?

GASENO: Your presence, my Lord, dignifies our humble meal.

BATRICIO: *(Aside)* As far as I'm concerned, your presence is a
            curse! But who am I to cause a fuss? Only the
            husband.

GASENO: Make room for our honoured guest.

DON JUAN: I'll sit here, if no-one objects.

Don Juan sits next to the bride.

BATRICIO: Sir! – that'd make you the bridegroom, if you sat there.

DON JUAN: God, I wish I was the bridegroom, if this peach is the bride!

BATRICIO: Sir, I am the bridegroom.

DON JUAN: Ah. I am in error. Still, never mind. *(Aside to Catalina.)* He seems a little off.

CATALINA: *(Aside to Don Juan.)* He's furious, poor chap! But what do you expect? With you leering at his wife? He's ruined and he knows it.

DON JUAN: *(Aside)* That's no reason not to be civil. – Madam, fortune has drawn me to the warm glow of your eyes – and already I am jealous of your husband.

AMINTA: Flatterer.

DON JUAN: Not at all. Mean every word.

BATRICIO: *(Aside)* Maria, I'm scared of him!

MARIA: *(Aside)* Why? What can he do? They're in full public view.

GASENO: Bring on the food! Let his Lordship eat.

BATRICIO: *(Aside)* A noble at our wedding. This bodes very, very ill.

Don Juan tries to take Aminta's hand.

DON JUAN: Don't pull it away.

AMINTA: Why not? It's my hand. Who do you think you are?

GASENO: More food! More food!

MARIA: And music!

Music strikes up. Don Juan takes Catalina aside.

DON JUAN: This one's rather tricky. What should I try?

CATALINA: I'd try and avoid a violent death at the hands of illiterate peasants, if I were you.

DON JUAN: But you're not. You're a coward.

CATALINA: A woman, actually.

DON JUAN: Not like this one. Look at her. Look at her fingers –
             delicate, white – I want to suck them, I'm burning
             inside!

CATALINA: She'll be burning inside by the time you've finished
             with her. She's trying not to glance this way. That
             means she's good and ripe. If you can get her alone I
             fear you'll succeed. Poor lamb!

DON JUAN: They're watching us! Their eyes are knives. Act
             normal, whilst I eat.

GASENO: Sing! Sing, for our children's happy day!

CATALINA: Yes, sing! *(Aside)* Soon you'll weep, and we'll be on our
             way.

             *Don Juan eats with the company, and flirts with the
             bride, who disdains him. The singers sing. Batricio
             speaks above them.*

BATRICIO: This jealousy is like a clock. Upon the hour it strikes,
             with perfect, mocking time, booming out a discord of
             your woe. On all the quarter-hours of chaos and the
             slow half-hours of pain, cracked chimes of grief and
             trouble in your heart. . . . My love's all twisted up. My
             joy has turned to pigswill. What does this pretty
             gentleman want? Does he enjoy my torture? I knew it
             was bad luck the minute he arrived. And sat straight
             down and flirted with my wife! Wouldn't even let me
             eat from my own plate at my own wedding! Arrogant
             bastard! Every time I tried to take a piece of meat –

DON JUAN: You don't want that.

BATRICIO: – he pushed my hand away –

DON JUAN: You'll get fat.

BATRICIO: – he said I was a glutton!

DON JUAN: How ill-bred.

BATRICIO: I turned to my mates, I said, what?!

SHEPHERD 1: What do you mean, what?

MARIA: Nothing to be frightened of.

SHEPHERD 2: They're all like that at court.

BATRICIO: What?

SHEPHERD 2:   It's the fashion.

BATRICIO: The fashion my arse! What sort of courtly custom is it, when a bridegroom starves while another man stuffs quails' eggs down his wife's long gurgling throat?

MARIA: They do things different in town.

BATRICIO: It profanes the blessed sacrament of marriage, that's what it does! *(Aside)* How can I bear the shame? My friends will think I'm feeble. Now the feast is over, and I never got a thing! Shite!

              Shepherds clear the feast. Exit all except Batricio and Don Juan.

              I suppose he's planning on joining us in bed, as well, is he? And when I have my woman, he'll tell me how vulgar I am, how ill-bred, what a right greedy pig! Well damn! I will be greedy if I want. She is mine, after all. Look out – master's coming – I'll duck down here –

DON JUAN: Batricio, my friend.

BATRICIO: *(Caught)* What can I do for your Lordship?

DON JUAN: I've got something to tell you.

BATRICIO: *(Aside)* Bad news.

DON JUAN: Earlier on today, Batricio, over lunch in fact, I vowed to devote myself to Aminta, body and soul, and really you should be the first to know that in return I have enjoyed –

BATRICIO: Her honour?

DON JUAN: . . . Yes.

BATRICIO: The secret places of her heart?

DON JUAN: Them too.

BATRICIO: *(Aside)* Clear proof of what I suspected. If she didn't love him all along, she would never have – Women are like that, sir.

DON JUAN: Oh, I don't know. Some are all right. Aminta's a good sort. But in the end her desperation at the thought of being chained to a brute shepherd and forced to live like cattle in some pigsty in the woods drove the sweet girl to write me this letter. Here, read it.

BATRICIO: I can't.

DON JUAN: Ah. Well look, to paraphrase, Aminta declares her everlasting love for, um, me, I'm afraid, Batricio, and the thing is, I thought it best if I gave you a chance, taking into account that I intend to experience the full range of delights promised herein, to preserve your manly honour.

BATRICIO: Bugger off, you mean.

DON JUAN: How astute.

BATRICIO: My choice is clear. Do what you like. I'll not be sniggered at behind my back. Women and a good name never go together, do they? Females are like bells – you judge them by their ring. And we all know the sound of a cracked bell, don't we? You have destroyed my life, Don Juan. But at least I have my honour. You enjoy her for a thousand years, sir. Sooner die broken-hearted, I would, than live to be deceived.

Exit Batricio.

DON JUAN: . . . Got him! Spiked on his own self-regard! Pathetic muck-stained peasants, clutching at their honour, little scrap of honour in the wind. . . ! That's how they think the world works. Money, no. Lust, no. Rank, no. Honour. Hah! Anyone with half a brain knows that honour only came to live in the village because it was so vilified in town. Now, for the final twist – before I do the damage, I'll bargain with the father, and get his full permission for the fraud. Night is coming down. I feel alive, every muscle fired with excitement! The trick goes well!

Enter Catalina bringing Gaseno.

CATALINA: Here's Gaseno, master.

DON JUAN: God be with you, old man.

GASENO: God be with you, Don Juan! Your servant says you wish to make a wonderful proposal!

DON JUAN: *(Kneels)* I should like to ask you, sir, for your daughter's hand in marriage. The boy Batricio has withdrawn – rather dishonourably in my estimation, but there you are, he is gone. And I have been smitten by the fair Aminta's charms. And I would take her as my wife.

GASENO: Was it love at first sight?

DON JUAN: It was.

GASENO: That's marvellous! She's yours! If you knew how rarely that happens down here – always a haggle about goats or wells or something. Let us go together and congratulate my daughter.

DON JUAN: Tomorrow. We'll go tomorrow. Tonight I've other plans.

GASENO: Till tomorrow, then!

DON JUAN: Goodnight. *(Exit Gaseno.)* Saddle the horses, Catalina. We leave at dawn.

CATALINA: I hope you haven't forgotten the minor matter of your other wedding – to Isabella? For heaven's sake, do this one quick, if you must do it at all!

DON JUAN: Of all the deceptions I've devised, this is the most delicious. A wedding night; no violence; entirely based on cunning!

CATALINA: Let's hope you don't get rumbled.

DON JUAN: What if I do? My father's Lord High Chamberlain, Chief Justice to the King.

CATALINA: That should come in handy, with a pitchfork up your bum.

DON JUAN: You're so afraid! It cripples you.

CATALINA: I'm afraid of God, and his vengeance. He damns those who rob others of their self-respect.

DON JUAN: Oh, does he?

CATALINA: Yes, he does! And he damns those who stand and
            watch, as well! I've stood silent far too often! I must be
            insane. I spend so much time dreading thunderbolts
            from heaven, I'm walking round with a crick in my
            neck! Don Juan, we shouldn't be here! These people
            don't deserve your hate – let's get out, before it's too
            late!

DON JUAN: You can leave if you want.

CATALINA: What, and live in a ditch, and eat berries? *(Pause)* I'll
            see to the horses.

DON JUAN: Good. Tomorrow we'll sleep in Seville.

CATALINA: Seville?

DON JUAN: Correct. Lebrija stinks of marriage.

CATALINA: But Seville will be up in arms against you, after your
            last outrage! Master, I think you overlook the fact that
            life's but one short step from death. It comes to
            everyone. Even you.

DON JUAN: Yes. But not yet. In the meantime, there's more
            mayhem to be wrought . . .

CATALINA: But sir –

DON JUAN: That's enough! Christ! You carp and cavil so much,
            my desire goes off! Be brave! You're nothing but a
            gutless girl.

CATALINA: Let the Turks be brave. Let the Scythians be brave,
            the Persians, the Galicians, the Japanese be brave! Let
            all the men in the world be brave! Where conscience is
            concerned, Catalina stays a coward.

            Exit Catalina. It's now dark.

DON JUAN: Black night drifts across the plains of Dos Hermanas.
            Stars shimmer in the heat. Now I go to work. Once
            I've got the scent of love, I follow, I'm bewitched. I'd
            risk the direst sentence for a girl with unlocked legs.
            The rank stench of a steaming bed, I never could
            resist! Aminta!

            Exit.

SCENE TWO

Aminta's bedroom. Enter Aminta and Maria.

MARIA: Now let's get you undressed and ready for your husband. Batricio will want you to look nice, won't he?

AMINTA: He'll be drunk.

MARIA: Only a little bit.

AMINTA: Maria, I'm sad.

MARIA: Every girl's sad on her wedding day.

AMINTA: But it's been such a cheerless wedding. Batricio's moping about like his whole flock had gone down with sheeprot. I've never seen him so melancholic! I blame that nobleman. What kind of chivalry is it, to sour my husband's heart? Oh, leave my hair, I'm not in the mood.

DON JUAN: *(Off)* Aminta. . . !

MARIA: There's Batricio calling. Pray God he's kind to you!

AMINTA: Go now, Maria.

MARIA: Remember, they like it if you make a bit of noise.

DON JUAN: *(Off)* Aminta. . . !

            Exit Maria.

AMINTA: Heaven turn my sighs to laughs, my tears to hot caresses. . . ! Come, Batricio.

            Enter Don Juan.

DON JUAN: It's not Batricio.

AMINTA: . . . Who is it then?

DON JUAN: Look close. Feel.

AMINTA: Oh God! I'm lost! What are you doing in my bedroom after dark?

DON JUAN: After dark is when I'm at my best.

AMINTA: Get out! I'll scream!

DON JUAN: Scream.

AMINTA: How dare you abuse the courtesy of our village? Batricio will sort you out. We have our gallants too, you know, here in Dos Hermanas!

DON JUAN: You're blushing.

AMINTA: Well of course I am!

DON JUAN: Let me say four words.

AMINTA: No! Get out! My husband's on his way!

DON JUAN: I am your husband.

AMINTA: . . . What?

DON JUAN: I am your husband.

AMINTA: Since when?

DON JUAN: Since the moment I saw you.

AMINTA: Who announced it?

DON JUAN: My desire.

AMINTA: Who blessed it?

DON JUAN: Your eyes.

AMINTA: My father will have something to say about this!

DON JUAN: He's already said it. He's agreed.

AMINTA: Impossible! Batricio cannot know.

DON JUAN: I'm afraid he does. He has forgotten you.

AMINTA: Forgotten me?

DON JUAN: Completely. It is I who adore you. And I swear I'll never leave.

AMINTA: You will. You will! Right now!

DON JUAN: Aminta – I have to have you or I'll die! I throw myself at your feet. Do what you want with me.

AMINTA: What a load of manure. Out!

DON JUAN: Listen! I am a gentleman of ancient family, heir to the house of Tenorio, conquistadors of Seville. My father sits at the King's right hand. His lips say life, or slaughter. As I was travelling along this road today, I chanced to see you smile. I was inflamed. I had to have you for my wife – without delay! I give you my name, Aminta. I give my hand in marriage. Take it. The King will disapprove – he's lined me up with someone else – some Duchess – in beauty, way beneath you, your inferior in love. My father will be angry; but I will suffer it. I must have you. I worship you. I must be your husband. Please!

AMINTA: I don't know what to say. I married Batricio. Even if he has deserted me, this knot cannot be broken. You know that.

DON JUAN: But your marriage is not consummated.

AMINTA: Sorry?

DON JUAN: You have not lain together, man and wife – have you?

AMINTA: Batricio would never dream of such behaviour!

DON JUAN: But you would. . . ?

AMINTA: I would not!

DON JUAN: Liar. The banns can be annulled. You are not married to Batricio. You are married to me. You want to be married to me. You love me.

AMINTA: It's true, he never kissed me . . .

DON JUAN: Well there you are. You're free. Take my hand. We'll pledge our love.

AMINTA: Are you having sport with me?

DON JUAN: Madam, I am too wary of my honour.

AMINTA: Then swear, by all that's holy, you'll keep your pledge.

DON JUAN: I swear on your baby-soft hand.

AMINTA: Swear to God, Don Juan, and may he curse you to hell if you break your promise.

DON JUAN: If by some hideous fluke I should be prevented from keeping my word, may God send me a terrible end at another man's hand – *(Aside)* providing he's deceased. From the live ones, saints preserve us!

AMINTA: You swear?

DON JUAN: I swear.

AMINTA: Then on that oath I am your wife.

DON JUAN: Come to my arms! My soul is yours.

AMINTA: My love. . . . My soul is yours . . .

DON JUAN: Then let me see you. Sweet, soft Aminta. Tomorrow
             you will walk in silver shoes, laced with gold. Your
             throat I will imprison in a manacle of rubies. Your
             fingers I will ring with glinting diamonds and pearls.

AMINTA: From this night, I am yours, I do your will . . .

DON JUAN: *(Aside)* You've just made the acquaintance of the
             trickster of Seville.

             Aminta is undressed. Blackout.

SCENE THREE

A road near Valencia. Enter Isabella, Don Pedro, and porters.

DON PEDRO: The sea is wild. I'm glad to be off that boat.

ISABELLA: Where have we landed?

DON PEDRO: Near Valencia. Rest a few days, then on to Seville.
             Happy?

ISABELLA: No, I am not.

DON PEDRO: But Seville, when you see Seville. . . ! The buildings
             are stylish; the food's the best in Europe; the girls are
             more desirable than any in the world. It's a highly
             sophisticated place! You'll soon forget your sorrows.

ISABELLA: Not until I discover the name of the thief who, with his
             faithless promise, stole the man I loved from me.

DON PEDRO: As I understand it, Duchess, you entered into a
             compact of your own free will. And now your title's
             bought you another chance, which you may or may not
             deserve. Be thankful for the magnanimity of Spain.

ISABELLA: I want Octavio!

DON PEDRO: Well, you have lost Octavio. But Don Juan Tenorio,

my nephew, is a most impressive catch. His reputation
is unblemished. His father's chief advisor to the King.

ISABELLA: Then why is he matched with me? I am worthless. I
weep for lost honour all the days of my life. Why am I
betrothed to this most excellent Don Juan?

DON PEDRO: Madam, I am but the escort. Your King knows best.
Cheer up! Tonight we'll get a glass of good Rioja.

ISABELLA: I don't want wine, I want Octavio!

Enter Tisbea, followed by Anfriso.

TISBEA: Sea of Spain, you spew up fire!

ANFRISO: It's all right.

TISBEA: I curse you to the very last drop! And I curse the
wind! And the boat that brought the havoc to our
shores!

ANFRISO: Don't panic.

ISABELLA: Why is she screaming so?

DON PEDRO: *(To Anfriso.)* Did you make this poor girl cry?

ISABELLA: Fisherwoman. Why do you rail at the sea?

TISBEA: Because it's wrecked my life, that's why! Look at it
steam and hiss! Monstrous thing!

ISABELLA: Tell me your story. Where are you from?

TISBEA: Further up the coast, ma'am. Tarragona. I lived in a
lovely little hut, whose walls gave shelter to a hundred
birds, that sang to me each dawn. I was hard as a
diamond, tucked away there. But then the ocean threw
fire at my house, and it melted my heart like wax!

ANFRISO: Are you bound for Valencia, sir?

DON PEDRO: Seville.

ISABELLA: I too know misfortune. Against my will, I shall be
married.

TISBEA: Ma'am, if my ruin stirs pity in your breast, let us go
with you. We too make for Seville, to petition the
King. I want justice. I want vengeance. Ma'am, I was

deceived! A Don Juan Tenorio was washed up on our
beach.

ISABELLA: Don Juan!

DON PEDRO: *(Aside)* I have a strange sinking feeling in my gut.

TISBEA: I nursed him, I cared for him, I brought him back to
life. And what did I get for my pains? My vile guest
turned to a viper, and slithered into bed! No woman
should ever trust a man! When he'd taken his pleasure,
he fled. You are a lady; you'll know the law. Tell me,
have I a case against the snake?

ISABELLA: Don Pedro, this –

TISBEA: Tisbea.

ISABELLA: – Tisbea is coming with us.

DON PEDRO: Why?

ISABELLA: Because I say so! She has been cruelly wronged.

DON PEDRO: But what can be done for it, Duchess?

ISABELLA: It's quite simple. She must marry your Don Juan. And
I must find Octavio. Come.

ANFRISO: *(Aside)* Before he marries my dear love, his blood will
stain the dust.

They exit.

SCENE FOUR

*Seville. A church, Catalina on her knees, muttering in Latin. Enter Don
Juan.*

CATALINA: Pray, Don Juan. We need all the help we can get.

DON JUAN: Why?

CATALINA: Why? Because Octavio's discovered what you did to
him in Naples, Isabella's being brought here to become
your lawful wife, and sooner or later the Marquis is
bound to reveal that he lent you his crimson –

DON JUAN: Enough! *(He hits her.)*

CATALINA: You broke my tooth.

DON JUAN: Keep your mouth shut, then. Where did you hear this rubbish?

CATALINA: It's not rubbish. It's the truth.

DON JUAN: The what?

CATALINA: The – oh I give up. You've no idea of good and bad at all. I'm leaving.

DON JUAN: . . . Don't go.

CATALINA: Why not?

DON JUAN: I hate to be alone. I'll double your wages.

CATALINA: You don't pay me wages.

DON JUAN: Tomorrow! I'll give you two thousand, tomorrow. Stay with me tonight. I need you. I don't even know where I'm lodging.

CATALINA: Round the back of the church. It's dark, and secret.

DON JUAN: What, sleep on consecrated ground?

CATALINA: A lot of people in Seville would love to get their hands on you. Here you should be safe. – When you say, stay with you. . . ?

DON JUAN: Yes?

CATALINA: In what sense, stay with you?

DON JUAN: In the stable, same as usual.

CATALINA: Oh. Right.

DON JUAN: Why, did you think you were getting the bed? I can't very well sleep with the horses, can I?

CATALINA: But you'll pay me tomorrow? *(Aside)* Enough to start out on my own?

DON JUAN: Catalina, I swear to you –

CATALINA: Don't do that, please. Just get the money.

DON JUAN: I promise. – Seen that boy from Dos Hermanas?

CATALINA: The bridegroom? Yes. He's sulking.

DON JUAN: Not surprised. *(Laughs)* Tremendous tactic. Played him off against himself. And I hear old Aminta's been running round town for a fortnight, trying to herd me up the aisle . . .

CATALINA: She now calls herself Countess Aminta. She thinks you'll keep your word.

DON JUAN: Does she really! Hah! – What's this?

CATALINA: It's the tomb of Don Gonzalo of Ulloa. The Commander you killed. Put up by order of the King.

DON JUAN: Very grand.

CATALINA: Makes me shiver.

DON JUAN: *(Reads the inscription.)* "Here lies a loyal and powerful Knight, trusting to the Lord for vengeance on the traitor that slew him." I like that. Quite poetic. Going to be revenged on me, are you, with your feet of stone? Your beard like a ridge on a mountain?

CATALINA: Don't pull it! That's sacrilege!

DON JUAN: Want to fight a duel, do you, Knight Commander of Calatrava? With your sword of chiselled rock? Then come to my lodging for supper tonight!

CATALINA: Come away. It's dark. Master! Come away!

DON JUAN: "Trusting to the Lord for vengeance". How quaint. If you're waiting for me to die, my friend, you'll be waiting a very long time. I'm young. I've years and years to spare! Come to dinner, if you dare!

They exit.

SCENE FIVE

Seville. The Alcazar. Enter Dona Anna, unkempt, and Don Diego.

DON DIEGO: Dona Anna. You wished to see me. – Are you unwell?

DONA ANNA: My vigil forbids me the niceties of dress.

DON DIEGO: Pardon me? Your vigil?

DONA ANNA: I do not sleep. I stalk the streets. I cultivate my
              powers.

DON DIEGO: *(Aside)* Unnatural frenzy . . .

DONA ANNA: I seek my father's killer!

DON DIEGO: My dear, we hold the murderer in chains, and be
              assured that due process of law will –

DONA ANNA: Wrong man! Wrong one!

DON DIEGO: But you said – in the crimson cloak –

DONA ANNA: He changed!

DON DIEGO: Anna, you need rest. Losing your father . . . a terrible
              shock. What about a few months in a nice convent?

DONA ANNA: No! I call to all my allies, come, convince them of their
              folly! Flutter, and crawl, and fill their brains with
              truth!

DON DIEGO: *(Aside)* This is sorcery! – Madam, they will burn you as
              a witch, if you –

DONA ANNA: Truth! I was not with Mota that night!

DON DIEGO: . . . Who were you with?

DONA ANNA: He had no name. Don Diego, your reputation is
              impeccable. I trust you to be discreet. Fetch the
              Marquis and set him before me. I will make him reveal
              what he knows.

DON DIEGO: . . . Very well. Stay here by the fountain.

              Exit Don Diego. Enter Aminta and Gaseno.

AMINTA: And this is the Alcazar, the great Moorish palace. This
              is where I'll live. See the tiles! I shall lounge around
              these courtyards in flowing silken robes. Eating figs.

GASENO: What's that? A statue?

AMINTA: A beggar, I think. Give her something.

GASENO: Here. Now hop it, you're spoiling the view.

DONA ANNA: Who are you?

GASENO: I am the father of my daughter. Her. I'm only an old
              shepherd, but she's about to be a Countess, and live

here, eating fruit. She won't speak to you. She's too posh. Now run along, get yourself a bowl of soup.

AMINTA: Father! Hurry! We must find Don Juan. I've heard he sometimes wanders in the gardens.

Exit Aminta.

DONA ANNA: Don Juan?

GASENO: Tenorio. He's the husband. We're so lucky! It's the biggest thing ever in Dos Hermanas!

Exit Gaseno. Enter Don Diego, with guards escorting the Marquis of Mota, in chains.

MOTA: Anna!

GUARD: On your knees!

DON DIEGO: Marquis. Sentence of death hangs over you. You have been questioned; you say you're innocent.

MOTA: I am innocent of every charge, except of love for this lady, which I freely admit, the torture's quite superfluous actually. But on my oath, I wasn't at her house!

DON DIEGO: She now corroborates your story.

MOTA: Thank God!

DON DIEGO: If you repent, you may be pardoned. But if it was not you – who was it?

MOTA: No idea.

DONA ANNA: Marquis – if you respect me –

MOTA: Oh, I do!

DONA ANNA: – and would have me respect you too –

MOTA: I would!

DONA ANNA: – tell us who borrowed your cloak.

DON DIEGO: The red cloak.

DONA ANNA: Who wore it?

DON DIEGO: Say.

MOTA: . . . There is a code of honour among men.

DONA ANNA: My father's dead!

MOTA: It was a joke –

DONA ANNA: My father's dead!

MOTA: I thought we were only diddling a whore!

DON DIEGO: Who's 'we'?

MOTA: I cannot say!

DON DIEGO: Come on, spit it out!

MOTA: I just cannot! – A friend!

DON DIEGO: A friend. Rather a predicament, yes I see that.

DONA ANNA: *(Aside)* Oh, the collusion!

MOTA: I really am sorry.

DONA ANNA: Don Diego, would you leave us for a moment?

DON DIEGO: Not permitted, I'm afraid.

DONA ANNA: But we're sweethearts. It's embarrassing.

DON DIEGO: Ah, I see.

Don Diego withdraws, smiling.

DONA ANNA: *(To Mota)* . . . I have something rather precious and I
             want to know if you want it. *(She kisses him hard.)* I
             have heat and moisture, spit and artistry. My fingers
             dawdle in forbidden places. My tongue knows several
             languages, including Arabic and French. My thighs
             can grip like wrestlers' arms, and lock our hips
             together. I'll lick the sweat from off your skin, from
             every crack and crevice. I'll be dirty. I like sin. I offer
             filthiness. You want it?

MOTA: Mmm . . .

DONA ANNA: Do you want it?

MOTA: Yes!

DONA ANNA: Give me a name!

MOTA: . . . Don Juan.

DONA ANNA: Don Juan.

Exit Dona Anna. Don Diego comes forward.

DON DIEGO: She is sad. She loved her father.

MOTA: Don Diego – your son, where is he now?

DON DIEGO: Banished, sir.

MOTA: Banished? I can't say I'm surprised.

DON DIEGO: Return the Marquis to his cell. I shall be speaking to the King.

Exit Mota and Guards.

My son is a wretch. I tried so hard. Where did he get it from?

Exit.

SCENE SIX

Don Juan's lodgings. Two servants set the table.

SERVANT 1: Everything better be perfect. Don Juan dines here tonight.

SERVANT 2: The table's laid – but where is he? The wine's getting hot and the food's getting cold. Someone should tell him to arrive on time.

SERVANT 1: Who would dare give orders to the crown prince of chaos?

Enter Catalina and Don Juan.

DON JUAN: Catalina, sit with me.

CATALINA: Sit with you?

DON JUAN: Sit with me. Serve dinner!

SERVANT 2: Right away, sir.

DON JUAN: What's the problem?

CATALINA: The soup. It's cold, and short of pepper. And the butter's on the turn.

DON JUAN: You're too fussy.

CATALINA: It's my trade.

DON JUAN: Tastes all right to me.

CATALINA: Everything tastes all right to you. You're totally
                undiscriminating. Unrefined of palate. Good food or
                poor, you just shovel it down, with a –

                A terrifyingly loud knock at the door.

                What's that?

DON JUAN: I think someone's at the door. – See who it is.

SERVANT 2:   Right away, sir.

                The Servant goes to the door.

CATALINA: What if they've come to arrest us?

DON JUAN: What if they have? You're so anxious! Eat.

                The Servant runs back in fright.

                Who is it? Don't just stand there quaking. Persuade
                your mouth to form itself into some kind of language.
                What did you see? The devil?

CATALINA: Probably.

DON JUAN: You go.

CATALINA: No thanks. Not in my contract.

DON JUAN: Less of the cheek! Now go!

CATALINA: They found my grandma strung up dead, hanging like
                a bunch of grapes. In the family we say she's been
                searching for her soul ever since. Wandering hither and
                thither through the ether. Now she'd have a knock like –

DON JUAN: What's the matter with you, Catalina?

CATALINA: I'm a coward. You know that.

DON JUAN: Are you going or not?

CATALINA: Not.

DON JUAN: You're fired. *(He takes her plate of food.)*

CATALINA: . . . I'll answer the door. – What if all the raped and
                ravished have come demanding vengeance?

                *Catalina goes to the door, and comes running back in
                fright.*

DON JUAN: Anyone we know?

CATALINA: God help me! He's got me! I'm done for!

DON JUAN: Who's got you? What did you see?

CATALINA: I saw a you know, a whassname, like a thingamejig from beyond, and it stared at me, and I – what's happened? I'm all of a muddle! – I opened the door and it, yes, 'who are you?' said the, and I run!

DON JUAN: Thank you so much. Lucid as ever. Have another glass of wine, see if things get any clearer. I'll go myself.

> *Don Juan goes to the door. The statue of Don Gonzalo enters. Don Juan retreats before it.*

CATALINA: What is it?

DON JUAN: It's the gentleman I invited to dinner. Sit down, sir. There's plenty of food. Bring some of your friends if you care to.

CATALINA: San Panuncio, San Anton! God protect us! What have we done? – Dead men like their grub, then, do they?

> *Don Gonzalo nods, and sits at the table.*

It nodded!

DON JUAN: Catalina, you sit too.

CATALINA: No thank you, master, I've had enough.

DON JUAN: You've barely started.

CATALINA: I'm full!

DON JUAN: Hopeless. Afraid of a dead man? How do you cope with the living? Sit down! – Superstitious peasant.

CATALINA: Master, you dine with your guest. To be honest I had rather a large lunch and I –

DON JUAN: Do you want me to lose my temper?

CATALINA: I can't sit down with you!

DON JUAN: Why not?

CATALINA: I'm too smelly!

DON JUAN: You're always smelly!

CATALINA: I just made a mess in my trousers!

DON JUAN: Christ preserve us. *(To the servants.)* And what's the matter with you two? Never seen a moving statue before? Twitching like a couple of halfwits.

CATALINA: I don't normally speak to strangers – do you really expect me to socialise with a lump of stone?

DON JUAN: If he's made of stone, what are you afraid of?

CATALINA: He might sit on my head!

DON JUAN: Be polite, then.

CATALINA: Oh . . . right. Er, how are you today – busy? Nice countryside, is it, where you come from? Sunny beaches? Gentle breeze? Do you play the lottery?

SERVANT 1:   It nods to every question!

CATALINA: Any good restaurants?

DON JUAN: Bring some wine!

CATALINA: And I suppose you get ice in your drinks, do you? Yes? Sounds pretty good to me.

DON JUAN: Perhaps our guest would care for some music?

SERVANT 2:   He said he would!

DON JUAN: Well sing, then, cretin!

CATALINA: The dead man has taste.

DON JUAN: Naturally. He's very well-bred.

SERVANTS: *(Sing)* Lady, you desire revenge
              Upon all faithless men;
              But only in death will they pay the price,
              And there's plenty of time till then.

CATALINA: Doesn't eat very much, does he? I'd try some of that ham if I could stop my teeth from chattering. Doesn't drink much, either. Tell you what – I'll drink for us both. *(Takes two glasses.)* I propose a toast: to the Man of Stone. Cheers. Cheers. For he's a jolly good fellow. Hip hip hooray. I feel my courage flooding back. – Do you know, I think we could get on very well together, you and I.

SERVANTS: *(Sing)* I only have one lifetime,
But I'm way, way off from death;
I mean to taste all the joys of love,
And there's plenty of time still left.

Lady, you desire revenge
Upon all faithless men;
But only in death will they pay the price,
And there's plenty of time till then.

CATALINA: You've double-crossed a lot of ladies, Don Juan – which one's the song about?

DON JUAN: *(Laughs)* All of them. Tonight, they get nothing but contempt.

Don Gonzalo bangs his fist on the table with a mighty crash.

I think he's finished. Clear the table, quick!

Don Gonzalo waves away everyone but Don Juan.

And then leave us alone.

CATALINA: Master, he's made of rock, you're only skin and bone – I don't like the look of it – don't stay!

DON JUAN: Out, the lot of you! Cowards! Away!

Exit Catalina and the Servants.

I'm at your service. What is it you want? What are you, a ghost? Do you walk the world in eternal pain? If I can relieve your sorrow, say how. I give my word I'll carry out whatever you command. Speak! Are you blessed, or did you die with all your sins upon you?

DON
GONZALO: How do I know you will keep your word as a gentleman?

DON JUAN: I will keep my word because I am a gentleman.

DON
GONZALO: Give me your hand. Don't be afraid.

DON JUAN: I'm not afraid. If you were the Devil himself I'd still give you my hand.

     They shake hands.

DON
GONZALO: By this contract, and your word, I expect you for dinner tomorrow at eight. Will you come?

DON JUAN: *(Aside)* My wedding night! – I'll come. I thought your orders would be more severe. Where?

DON
GONZALO: My chapel.

DON JUAN: Alone?

DON
GONZALO: No, bring your servant. Will you honour this vow?

DON JUAN: I swear on the name of Tenorio.

DON
GONZALO: I swear on the name of Ulloa.

DON JUAN: I'll be there. I am a man.

DON
GONZALO: I was a man, and I believe you. *(Turns to go.)*

DON JUAN: Shall I send for a light to see you home?

DON
GONZALO: No. God's grace is light enough.

     Exit Don Gonzalo, slowly.

DON JUAN: Dear God! I'm dripping sweat! I'm roasting! Dreadful heat! Yet deep inside, my heart's a block of ice! When he took my hand in his, his grip, it was so terrible, I thought I was in hell – and his breath was freezing, biting cold, a bitter day in winter! But stop. The human imagination is a powerful thing. Simple fear is fair enough. But fear of dead bodies is altogether vulgar. I wasn't afraid of him whilst he lived. I shall not be awed by him dead. Tomorrow I'll attend this little soirée at his tomb, and my bravery will dazzle all Seville!

     Exit.

SCENE SEVEN

The Alcazar. Don Pedro is waiting. A lady passes by. He bows to her, with a wink. She exits. He laughs. Enter Don Diego.

DON DIEGO: Pedro!

DON PEDRO: Brother! I'm home! Seville never seemed more lovely, than on return from years abroad. What's the news?

DON DIEGO: The city is a cesspool of intrigue. My son is at its centre.

Enter the King of Castile. They bow.

KING OF
CASTILE: You are welcome, Don Pedro, though your information is not. The Italian Duchess is opposing our intent? Why, what did you tell her?

DON PEDRO: Sire, she is merely racked by shame and slander. She does not know Don Juan brought on her fall.

KING OF
CASTILE: She need not know.

DON PEDRO: I took that view.

KING OF
CASTILE: Nevertheless, the boy's behaviour is scandalous.

DON PEDRO: His bravado is the mark of immaturity. He'll make a useful envoy when his youthful wings are clipped. Allow him one more chance, Sire; marriage, children, and career will see the end of his mischief.

KING OF
CASTILE: Quite right. High time he grew up. The wedding shall proceed as planned. And make a proclamation: from this day forth Don Juan shall be titled Count of Lebrija, and shall live and govern there, as our right hand.

DON DIEGO: Sire, you are merciful! *(Aside to Don Pedro.)* I thank you for your intercession, brother.

KING OF
CASTILE: Now. Dona Anna of Ulloa. Let's get everything
shipshape. We'll have her paired off as well, shall we?
With this Octavio?

DON DIEGO: If I might venture to intervene. . . ? *(Calls)* Bring him
in.

> *Guards lead in the Marquis of Mota. Unnoticed,*
> *Tisbea sneaks in as well, and tries to get near to the*
> *King.*

Dona Anna begs a pardon for the Marquis of Mota.
She swears it was not he that took advantage of her
honour, but one who, adopting a disguise of some
adroitness, slipped in and then out in his stead.

DON PEDRO: *(Laughs)* Hah!

DON DIEGO: May I finish, Pedro? – And this same man killed her
father.

DON PEDRO: *(Aside)* Hell! Turned assassin? I didn't know that. God
forgive me – what have I let loose?

DON DIEGO: In conclusion, I suggest Your Highness might consider
joining Anna not to Octavio, but to the Marquis, for
they have each been sorely wronged, and are I think in
love.

KING OF
CASTILE: In love? How unusual. You counsel well, Don Diego. I
authorise this match. Marquis – ?

MOTA: Sire, I vow to live a decent life, and be a faithful
husband.

KING OF
CASTILE: Good. Make ready for church.

DON PEDRO: Sire, will you excuse me? Urgent business in the town.

> *They bow. Don Pedro, Mota and Guards exit. Tisbea*
> *seizes her chance.*

TISBEA: *(Timidly)* Sire –

> *Enter Octavio and Ripio. Tisbea hangs back.*

OCTAVIO: I greet Your Highness face down on the floor!

KING OF
CASTILE: *(Aside)* Italians.

OCTAVIO: Sire, I have come to beg a favour.

KING OF
CASTILE: Should it contribute to good order, it is yours.

OCTAVIO: I saw your ambassador leaving. He must have told you
              what the world, it seems, already knows, for I learnt
              this from gossips: that with typical Spanish vanity and
              arrogance, some time ago in Naples, a noble lady's
              honour was befouled by one Don Juan.

KING OF
CASTILE: Yes. And – ?

OCTAVIO: I ask your permission to challenge him to a duel.

DON DIEGO: No, Your Majesty! Forbid it!

KING OF
CASTILE: Duke Octavio, Don Juan has been elevated to high
              position at court. He is a branch of our royal tree. I can
              hardly permit his hacking off, now, can I?

OCTAVIO: No, Sire.

KING OF
CASTILE: So a duel is quite out of the question. No.

OCTAVIO: Naturally I must obey. I withdraw, and ask your pardon.

KING OF
CASTILE: Splendid chap! You too shall be married soon. Don
              Diego, attend me.

              Exit the King and Don Diego.

OCTAVIO: *(Aside)* Married? Who to? This Dona Anna, who'll
              copulate with anyone in red? I count all women false
              and superficial now. The only one I ever loved was
              Isabella. But she goes to the man who debauched her –
              Don Juan!

TISBEA: Don Juan? Don Juan's the one that brought down
              Isabella?

OCTAVIO: Who are you?

TISBEA: Another that was ruined by this smooth-tongued libertine. I must tell the Duchess, before she marries him!

OCTAVIO: She's here?

Enter Aminta and Gaseno.

GASENO: This gentleman may know. – Sir, we are looking for Don Juan Tenorio. Have you seen him?

OCTAVIO: Don Juan Tenorio?

GASENO: That's the boy.

OCTAVIO: Why are you after him?

AMINTA: 'Cause he's my husband, sir.

TISBEA: Your husband?

GASENO: Aminta's a good Christian and comes with a dowry.

AMINTA: I was a virgin, too.

GASENO: All my land, sheep, goats, pigs, ducks, dogs and chickens.

AMINTA: He made me a promise!

TISBEA: He made me a promise.

AMINTA: What did he promise you?

TISBEA: Love and honour and all the rest.

AMINTA: That's what he said to me!

TISBEA: That's what he's said to lots of us.

AMINTA: What?

OCTAVIO: Don Juan is a deceiver.

AMINTA: What?

TISBEA: He'll promise any treasure to get what he desires.

AMINTA: *(Weeping)* He loves me!

TISBEA: *(Gently)* No. He loves no-one but himself.

GASENO: I thought so all along . . .

AMINTA: Villain! Where is he? I'll rip out his giblets and feed them to the pigs! I'll geld him with a rusty knife! He's made a fool of me. . . !

TISBEA: Come. We will share our sad stories, and plot our revenge.

GASENO: Yes, I had my suspicions . . .

Exit Tisbea, Aminta and Gaseno.

OCTAVIO: Don Juan, I may not fight you, yet I have no doubt this disorder cannot be. Your time is running out.

Exit.

SCENE EIGHT

Seville. Night. Enter Catalina.

CATALINA: My master's with the King. Being raised to the peerage. He went in a rascal, he'll come out a Count. It's standard practice here. And tonight he's actually going through with a wedding! I suspect the King's twisted his arm. But when do I get my two thousand, that's what I want to know. . . ? He said tomorrow. Well, this is tomorrow. I've been living for tomorrow for as long as I recall. I'll buy a little corner bar, serve the best chilled soup in Seville! All you have to do is get a reputation, and you're rich, and once you're rich, you can live off your reputation.

Enter Don Pedro.

DON PEDRO: You! Have you seen Don Juan?

CATALINA: Who, sir?

DON PEDRO: Never mind.

Exit Don Pedro.

CATALINA: The more I think about it, the more I think I'm ripe for a change of career. This job's dangerous. All that lust and dissipation has left my nerves in shreds. But nonetheless, I love to watch him move . . .

Enter Dona Anna.

DONA ANNA: Dark spirits, guide me to his lair. . . . I'm searching for Don Juan Tenorio.

CATALINA: I don't know what he looks like.

DONA ANNA: Nor I. I know only his voice.

CATALINA: Sorry. They all sound the same to me.

DONA ANNA: If you lie, I'll put a spell on you. I'll turn you to a toad.

CATALINA: What are you, a witch? Go away!

DONA ANNA: Might he be in Cantarranas?

CATALINA: What for? He gets married tonight.

DONA ANNA: *(Aside)* So! Perfect formation of the stars! I have the key to him. – Then my hunt is ended, and I leave him to his wife.

Exit Dona Anna, sobbing.

CATALINA: I wouldn't sniff at the responsibilities of marriage myself. In a place of my own, doing a healthy trade, little white apron, I'd say I'd be rather attractive. . . . Surely someone'll make me an offer? One day Don Juan will be gone. Without him to measure up to, perhaps the rest won't seem so dull.

Enter Anfriso.

ANFRISO: I know you.

CATALINA: Most unlikely.

ANFRISO: Yes I do, I know you. You were with that bastard when he washed up on our beach.

CATALINA: Anfriso! It's been ages! How are you keeping?

ANFRISO: He's not getting my Tisbea!

CATALINA: I don't think he wants your Tisbea. But he asked me to give you a message.

ANFRISO: A message?

CATALINA: Yes. He'd like you to meet him at dawn tomorrow, down by the docks, to sort the whole thing out.

ANFRISO: Dawn. At the docks. Well, you tell him from me, I be fast with my filleting knife!

Exit Anfriso.

CATALINA: Why can't he lead a normal life? My big, brave beautiful boy? Set up with one good woman, and abandon this urge to destroy?

Enter Don Juan, in a sash.

A very good day, Count of Lebrija, your worship. I trust His Majesty received you graciously?

DON JUAN: Considerably more lovingly than my own father.

CATALINA: And the wedding's still on for tonight?

DON JUAN: *(Gloomily)* Yes.

CATALINA: *(Aside)* That's a relief! – Let's go home and get suitably dressed.

DON JUAN: No. It'll have to wait. I've another appointment.

CATALINA: What's that?

DON JUAN: Dinner with the Dead Man.

CATALINA: Don't be a damn fool!

DON JUAN: I gave my word.

CATALINA: You don't have to keep your promise to a ghost!

DON JUAN: And what if it gets around town? My good name would be worthless.

CATALINA: You're insane!

DON JUAN: I trust him. He's a gentleman. He invited me for dinner, and I'm going, and you're coming too.

CATALINA: That was a warning. Do you wish to die?

DON JUAN: No harm will befall us. I've shaken his hand. Besides, I can get married any time. This is something different.

They exit. Dona Anna emerges from a hiding place and follows them.

SCENE NINE

The Alcazar. Isabella is dressed in a white wedding gown by a maid.

ISABELLA: So this is the price of pleasure. One slip, and life comes to an end. Once I was an object of desire; men went on their knees to me, paraded me through patios, observed me as I bathed. . . . I had such power! From tonight, I am a sow that breeds, abandoned in a courtyard, my beauty veiled from all men's sight. I shall grow old and bitter on some Andalucian farm. Society has shut its doors; all gaiety's forbidden. I shall wear black for ever, to remind me of the night I was undone. Who was the man who cheated me? Which one?

MAID: You will never know. Be calm, madam. Accept your life, it is God's plan.

ISABELLA: Amen.

Enter Tisbea and Aminta.

Tisbea! Did you get to the King?

TISBEA: No. But I got to Duke Octavio.

ISABELLA: Octavio!

TISBEA: He's in Seville.

ISABELLA: Send for him!

MAID: No man may enter in these rooms. You stay here now till marriage.

TISBEA: Octavio knows who is the cause of all our sorrow. Don Juan.

ISABELLA: Don Juan? But I marry Don Juan tonight, despite my protestations!

TISBEA: Two Kings have made a pact. We are bartered like livestock. This is Aminta, a friend. She too has suffered from his mischief.

AMINTA: I had fifteen days of greatness, so I thought, and loved every minute of it, ma'am. Now I'm nothing again. That's the meanest trick that ever was. To taste life, and then lose it.

ISABELLA: To taste life, and then lose it . . . . unkind truth. Every day, when others pray, I weep.

TISBEA: And so do I.

AMINTA: I see my future now: a cabin with walls of mud.

ISABELLA: I see white walls, red flowers, incandescent in the heat; an oak door stoutly fastened; a well to hold my tears.

TISBEA: I will pursue him till I'm old and grey. I have no other purpose.

Enter Dona Anna.

DONA ANNA: I know where he is!

ISABELLA: Don Juan?

DONA ANNA: Don Juan! I know where he is!

TISBEA: How do you know we seek him?

DONA ANNA: Every woman seeks him. He has a bill to pay. Come on! He's hidden in a church!

AMINTA: I'll kill him!

Exit all.

SCENE TEN

Don Gonzalo's chapel. It's dark. Don Juan and Catalina enter. The Commander's tomb is before them. They approach.

CATALINA: Almighty God, send me safely from this church, I'll never tell fibs again. Wah! Something moved.

DON JUAN: Do shut up. – Who's there?

Don Gonzalo enters.

DON
GONZALO: It is I.

CATALINA: Oh Lord, Oh Lord, I'm dead!

DON
GONZALO: I did not think you'd keep your word, Don Juan. You haven't with anyone else.

DON JUAN: Are you calling me a coward?

DON
GONZALO: The night you murdered me, you ran away.

DON JUAN: I could hardly wait round to be recognised. However, here we are. What do you want of us?

DON
GONZALO: I invited you to dinner.

CATALINA: I'm afraid we can't possibly accept. You haven't got a kitchen. We don't eat salad after dark.

DON
GONZALO: The ovens are under the tombstone. Raise it.

> *Don Juan does so. An infernal feast is revealed.*

How strong you are!

DON JUAN: Runs in the blood.

CATALINA: The table-top's as black as tar.

DON
GONZALO: Please sit.

> *Two cadaverous servants dressed in black enter with chairs. Catalina hesitates.*

DON
GONZALO: Sit!

CATALINA: Sir, I've got a bit of an upset tummy, to tell you the –

DON
GONZALO: Sit!

CATALINA: . . . I've sat.

DON
GONZALO: Impertinence!

CATALINA: Sorry. *(Aside)* San Panuncio, San Anton, get me out of here! – What's this, then? The *plat du jour?*

DON
GONZALO: A dish of snakes in venom.

CATALINA: And the garnish?

DON
GONZALO: Scorpions' spit.

CATALINA: Really? What do you do, do you marinade the –

DON
GONZALO: It's the speciality of the house.

CATALINA: I see. Trade secret. The casserole?

DON
GONZALO: Fingernails.

CATALINA: Sharp, and curved like talons: a solicitor?

DON
GONZALO: Won't you try some?

DON JUAN: . . . I'll try anything.

DON
GONZALO: I have music for you, too.

> *Don Gonzalo signals, and a horrible, ghoulish band of
> the damned come on, and play weird instruments, and
> sing to an unearthly tune . . .*

CATALINA: Do you have a decent cellar? Any good wine laid
            down?

DON
GONZALO: Taste. *(Pours wine.)*

CATALINA: A complex bouquet. Got quite a nose on it, hasn't it?
            Let me guess: vinegar, phlegm, and donkeys' piss?

DON
GONZALO: Our finest vintage, yes.

BAND OF THE
DAMNED: *(Sing)* Every man, take warning:
            God sees all you do.
          · He sees the debts you leave unpaid.
            He means to punish you.

CATALINA: It's pretty bad news, Don Juan – we're for the chop!

DON JUAN: My blood has turned to ice.

BAND OF THE
DAMNED: *(Sing)* Every man, live decently,

> And do not dare to boast
> There's "plenty of time to pay your debts";
> For if you do, you'll roast!

DON JUAN: I've eaten all I can, Don Gonzalo.

DON
GONZALO: You've tried everything?

DON JUAN: Yes. Everything.

DON
GONZALO: Then give me your hand.

DON JUAN: Why?

DON
GONZALO: It is time. Give me your hand. Are you frightened?

DON JUAN: No, I'm not frightened.

DON
GONZALO: Then give me your hand.

DON JUAN: You are a gentleman . . .

DON
GONZALO: I am. Give me your hand.

DON JUAN: *(Screams)* Aaah! I'm burning! You said it was safe!

DON
GONZALO: I did not.

DON JUAN: You tricked me! Your hand's red-hot! I'm on fire!

DON
GONZALO: Nothing compared with the heat that is to come; that you've sought for so long. God demands your debt be repaid! You failed to heed His warning. Now His mercy turns to justice. Every man pays, for every sin!

DON JUAN: Let go! I'll stab you! – The dagger glances off! I cannot cut through stone!

CATALINA: Master!

DON JUAN: I'm trapped! I burn!

DON
GONZALO: For ever.

DON JUAN: I did not seduce your daughter – she caught me just in time!

DON
GONZALO: No matter. You tried.

DON JUAN: Get me a priest! I want to confess!

DON
GONZALO: No priest can save you now. No holy water. No donations . . .

> *Don Juan and Catalina are despatched to the lower regions. The church doors burst open and Isabella, Tisbea, Aminta and Dona Anna enter.*

DON JUAN: I'm burning! The hands of devils clutch at me! I'm burning! Aaaah!

CATALINA: Me too! Must I die for serving him? I only did what I was told!

DON JUAN: Help me! Help me, please!

ISABELLA: Should we?

AMINTA: Let him go.

DON JUAN: The flames!

DON
GONZALO: Witness the justice of the Lord!

> *They sink out of sight into hell. Don Gonzalo becomes a statue once again. At the last moment Tisbea runs forward and grabs Catalina.*

TISBEA: Catalina!

> *Isabella helps haul Catalina to safety. Enter Don Pedro.*

DONA ANNA: He's gone.

AMINTA: Yes. I hope to God he never comes back.

DONA ANNA: He'll only come if we invite him.

ISABELLA: Who is this?

CATALINA: His servant. If I could tell you what I've seen. . . !

TISBEA: Tell us.

CATALINA :   Some time ago we came across the tomb of Don
              Gonzalo –

DONA ANNA : My poor father.

CATALINA :   – who Don Juan wickedly killed. And Don Juan
              mocked the statue. He pulled its granite beard. Invited
              it to dinner. And do you know what? It came. And
              after it had eaten, it returned the invitation. So my
              master and I dined here tonight, and after we had
              eaten, it took his hand, and squeezed. Then the earth
              opened under us. We saw the mouth of hell. It's really
              true. It's really there. I've never been so frightened. I
              only looked on, when Don Juan sinned. But that's
              enough to damn me. He fought, but the stone man was
              too strong. The rest you saw. Don Juan is gone. And
              God spared me to tell you. That every man pays, for
              every sin. That justice will be done.

AMINTA :   What happens now, without him?

ISABELLA :   I return to the Alcazar. I am a widow! Octavio is mine.
              Come with me, all of you. I will see you well
              apportioned.

AMINTA :   What, with Batricio?

TISBEA :   Anfriso?

DONA ANNA : The dissolute Marquis?

TISBEA :   Isabella – have you ever *met* the Duke Octavio?

              Don Pedro comes forward and kneels at the altar.

CATALINA :   Who are you, sir?

DON PEDRO : Don Juan's uncle.

CATALINA :   His uncle? He spoke highly of you.

DON PEDRO : Did he? That makes it worse. *(Prays)* Almighty Lord, I
            beg forgiveness. Tell me how I may atone, and be a
            better man.

CATALINA :   Sir, I don't like to mention it, but that nephew of yours
              owed me a couple of thousand. . . . I'm starting out in
              trade. . . .

DON PEDRO : Kneel.

CATALINA: Should we pray?

DON PEDRO: Every day. For our souls. We should pray.

All bow their heads. Slow fade.

THE END

FURTHER PLAYS AVAILABLE FROM ABSOLUTE CLASSICS

PAINS OF YOUTH

Ferdinand Bruckner
Translated by Daphne Moore

'Discovery of the Year'
GUARDIAN

£4.95

A FAMILY AFFAIR

Alexander Ostrovsky
Adapted by Nick Dear

'a stinging and scurrilously funny version by Nick Dear'
OBSERVER

£4.95

THUNDER IN THE AIR

August Strindberg
Translated by Eivor Martinus

'a sulphurous, atmospheric work full of summer lightning'
GUARDIAN

£4.95

TURCARET

Alain-René Lesage
Translated/adapted by John Norman

'One of the best of French comedies'
SUNDAY TELEGRAPH

£4.95

THE POWER OF DARKNESS

Leo Tolstoy
Translated/adapted by Anthony Clark

'THE POWER OF DARKNESS rends the air with greatness'
SPECTATOR

£4.95

ANATOL
Arthur Schnitzler
Translated by Michael Robinson

'*Schnitzler's most amusing and original play*'
DAILY TELEGRAPH

£4.95

THERESE RAQUIN
Emile Zola
Translated by Pip Broughton

'*A gripping yarn*'
GUARDIAN

£4.95

FALSE ADMISSIONS, SUCCESSFUL STRATEGIES, LA DISPUTE
Marivaux
Translated by Timberlake Wertenbaker

'*the most successful English translator of Marivaux in the present age, if not ever*'
OBSERVER

£5.95

FUENTE OVEJUNA, LOST IN A MIRROR
Lope de Vega
Adapted by Adrian Mitchell

'*It is hard to imagine a more gripping tale than the one which emerges in Adrian Mitchell's translation*'
TIME OUT

£5.95

THE LIAR, THE ILLUSION
Pierre Corneille
Translated/adapted by Ranjit Bolt

Two contrasting plays from one of France's major classic playwrights in an elegant new translation.

£.5.95

MAN, BEAST AND VIRTUE
Luigi Pirandello
A new version by Charles Wood

'There's no doubting the brilliance of this 1919 farce'
INDEPENDENT

£4.95

FORTHCOMING TITLES

THE GREAT HIGHWAY
August Strindberg
Translated by Eivor Martinus

Published April 1990

£4.95

BERENICE
Racine
LE MISANTHROPE, THE SCHOOL FOR WIVES
Molière
Adapted by Neil Bartlett

Published May 1990

£5.95

SARA
Translated by Ernest Bell
MINNA VON BARNHELM
Translated by Anthony Meech
Gotthold Lessing

Published April 1990

£5.95

NANA
Adapted by Olwen Wymark
GERMINAL
Adapted by William Gaminara
From the novels of Emile Zola

Published June 1990

£5.95